Mary's Life in the Spirit

Meditations on a Holy Duet

Mary's Life in the Spirit

Meditations on a Holy Duet

George T. Montague, SM

Published by The Word Among Us Press
7115 Guilford Drive
Frederick, MD 21704

15 14 13 12 11   1 2 3 4 5

ISBN: 978-1-59325-192-5
eISBN: 978-1-59325-414-8

Cover design by John Hamilton Designs
Front Cover Photo Credit: Jan van Eyck, c.1390-1441.
The Ghent altar—Polyptych with the Adoration of the Lamb, 1432.
The Virgin Mary of the Annunciation, from the center of the workday panels.
Location: Cathedral of St. Bavo, Ghent, Belgium
Photo Credit: Erich Lessing/Art Resource, NY

Made and printed in the United States of America

Library of Congress Cataloging-in-Publication Data
Montague, George T.
Mary's life in the Spirit : meditations on a holy duet / George T. Montague.
    p. cm.
ISBN 978-1-59325-192-5
1. Mary, Blessed Virgin, Saint--Meditations. 2. Holy Spirit—Meditations.
3. Catholic Church—Prayers and devotions. I. Title.
    BX2160.23.M66 2011
    232.91--dc22
                        2011016223

Contents

Introduction

The Song of Mary and the Spirit

Resting against a eucalyptus tree, you survey a lush green valley that runs like a carpet to a stairway of foot-hills. Your eyes climb the stairs to encounter a wall of snow-gowned mountains, high enough to challenge the jet routes. You feast on what the locals call "the dwellings of the gods," the Himalayas.

You are in an October Nepal.

Before you take many breaths, your peaceful silence is broken by the bold song of the Himalayan barbet, a bright-green, dove-sized bird with scarlet underparts. As you listen intently, another song reaches your ears, as loud and as beautiful, but very different from the first. It is the female barbet singing her response. They continue to serenade each other—and you, as if to welcome you to the valley.

In the depth of the Trinity, there is such a duet, Father and Son, singing their mutual love, so perfect that the song itself is the Person of the Holy Spirit. But the divine Persons are not lost in solitary splendor. By their own free and loving choice, their song goes out and touches a human ear, as the barbets' duet touched yours. The song came first to the ear, then to the heart, of a teenage girl in an obscure village called Nazareth. Would she not only hear the song but also learn it? Would she hear its invitation to be its mouthpiece, its yes from the yes of the Trinity? "*Fiat,* let it be," Mary said. And through the Holy Spirit, her life became the Trinitarian duet in human tones. The song entered her mind when she questioned, her heart when she agreed, her womb when she consented. And the Word became flesh. When she arose from her prostration before the miracle, her life continued the song.

This book is about the duet that the Holy Spirit continues to sing with Mary. It assumes an intimate union of the Holy Spirit with her. Their harmony invites us to the garden of the King. The Spirit and the bride say, "Come" (Revelation 22:17). I invite you to walk with me in this garden and cherish each scene of Mary's life and inhale there the fragrance of the Holy Spirit.

The Gospel Symphony

This is a book of meditative art. Those who know me for my biblical studies will be surprised, perhaps, by the approach of this book. I have spent much of my life in careful scientific study of the Scriptures, using the historical-critical method as a basis for what theological reflections it suggests or permits. However, this book is more a work of art than science, since in it I attempt to do in prose what painters and playwrights for two millennia have done with scenes from the Bible. Those scenes are skeletal texts that artists seek to bring to life by filling in the gaps. Thus, in Rembrandt's famous scene of the father embracing his prodigal son, we see a wealth of detail that led Henri Nouwen to write an entire book about the painting, *The Return of the Prodigal Son.* And in dramatizing Jesus' passion, Christians have done the same. In *The Passion of the Christ,* a film that had great impact on world audiences, Mel Gibson enhanced the basic story line with settings and additional scenes. So as I reviewed the few gospel scenes in which Mary plays a part, I have allowed my imagination to fill in the gaps in the same way that an artist might, while doing my best to be faithful to the general outline of the text.

Even the gospels themselves are works of art. This is not to say that they are not history; after all, a portrait of you will not look like someone else. But alternate portraits will differ in detail. Each Evangelist has put together his materials in an artistic way to help you identify with Jesus. The arrangement of the scenes, the plot, the characters, the settings, and other narrative tools tell us a lot about the theology of the Evangelist, that is, his particular take on the story of Jesus. Thus, in Matthew, Jesus appears especially as teacher; in Mark, as the hero who gives himself up to a sacrificial death; in Luke, as healer; in John, as the revealer of the Father. The Church listens to all of these voices as if to a symphony in which each instrument offers its own beautiful sound. This theological artistry is particularly true of the infancy gospels, which supply us with most of the narrative about Mary. The stories they tell are aimed primarily at affirming truths about Jesus, his divinity and his mission, and in regard to Mary, at showing her as the ideal responder and collaborator in God's saving plan. They invite us to enter the drama and experience the revelation.

In studying individual gospels, biblical scholars tend to wear earphones so that they can listen to a particular gospel without hearing the accompaniment of the others. Well and good.

But the Church listens to the symphony. And it is for that reason that I take the liberty of coalescing the infancy stories when necessary to follow the timeline of Jesus' infancy. For example, Luke tells us that after Joseph and Mary have presented Jesus in the temple, they retire to Nazareth. But Matthew indicates that they spend some time in Bethlehem, long enough to let the Magi arrive and for Herod to plot to kill all the children up to the age of two. To tell the complete story of Jesus' early years, we must insert Matthew's account of the Magi and the massacre of the infants after Joseph and Mary have presented Jesus in the temple. This is, indeed, to run the risk of skewing Luke's portrait of the infancy. But we must keep in mind that the Church reads the Bible as one book, with an overarching theme that transcends the individual parts. When the Church put the parts together in the canon, she was saying that she is the ultimate and authoritative reader of the entire book. It is this ultimate level that is the finished work of the Holy Spirit.

The Church invites us to enter that world, to listen to all the instruments in this symphony and allow the whole to transform our lives. Just as a symphony may invite us in turn to focus at one time on the flutes, then the violins, then the French horns, and so on, so can we enjoy each book of the Bible in its own right, but we do not isolate it from the whole canon. So in the meditations that follow, I seek to plumb each passage that sheds light on the relation of Mary and the Holy Spirit, enjoying it in the narrative world in which it is placed and hearing in the background the accompaniment of the rest of Scripture. I am fully aware that the gospels view the life of Jesus, and particularly the stories of Jesus' birth and infancy, in the light of the resurrection, and thus certain titles and events are described in ways that anticipate their full meaning, which will be revealed only later. Such was the choice of the Evangelists, but they nevertheless invite us to enter the world of the text as it stands.

Filling In the Gaps

What I do here—allowing my imagination to fill in the gaps left in the Scriptures to invite reflection—is a pondering of the kind that Mary herself did (Luke 2:19). But I do so within limits. I am a bit like a child who uses his imagination to color the drawings in a sketchbook but always does his best to stay within the lines. I do my best to stay within the lines drawn by the Scriptures. And as I reflect on the Scriptures, I do so in the light of the two thousand years of the Church's reflection on Mary and, therefore, also of those Marian truths that allow us to see Mary in the gospels as immaculately conceived and with a holiness and a mission that destines her to share Jesus' risen glory in the assumption. However, none of these truths remove the night of faith in which she walks with us, nor the questions that must have baffled her in her life's journey. Being fully docile to the Holy Spirit meant living with the questions in a deep faith that was all the more meritorious because it didn't have the answers—yet.

Three other comments about my method are in order. First, for scenes in which Joseph is present, my zoom lens focuses on Mary rather than on the foster father of Jesus. Much could be written about Joseph's own spiritual pilgrimage, and especially about his modeling of fatherhood, but our concern here is Mary and her relation to the Holy Spirit.

Second, though we are focusing on Mary and the Holy Spirit, we never lose sight of Jesus. We are just seeing him through Mary's eyes. I once saw a painting of a woman's eye that reflected three crosses, the central and larger one being the crucified Son, and from the woman's eye, a tear was falling. The artist was inviting us to view the suffering Jesus in the eye of his mother. Jesus reflected in Mary is Jesus enhanced.

Third, when referring to the Holy Spirit, I use the referential pronoun "he." I am not perfectly comfortable with that because the Greek word for "spirit," *pneuma,* is neuter—and that's why the New American Bible often uses "it." And, moreover, the Holy Spirit manifests many feminine traits. The Hebrew word for "spirit," *ruah,* is mostly feminine. In Lithuanian, "spirit" is feminine, as I learned in conversing with a young Lithuanian who in his broken English kept referring to the Holy Spirit as "she." I don't think "it" is suitable for the Person of the Holy Spirit, and I hesitate to call the Spirit "she" because of the confusion it might cause for traditional Christians. I hope this brief discussion, however, will help the reader understand that our gendered language about God is metaphorical. The difference between our human experience and God is greater than the likeness, and yet we have to use words when talking about a reality that infinitely surpasses words.

George T. Montague, SM

Chapter I

Perfect Pilgrim

Awoman went to church to take her burdens to prayer. A workman in the choir loft, thinking he would have some fun, called out in a booming voice: "I am Jesus, the Lord." To which the woman answered, "Hush! I'm talking to your mother."

Here's another story: A girl, a troublemaker at school and home, kept pestering her mother for a red bike for her tenth birthday. "Do you think you deserve it?" her mom asked. "Of course I do!" she snapped. "Well, why don't you ask God about that?" her mother replied. The girl stomped upstairs, sat down, and started to write a letter to God. But finding no way to tell God that she deserved the bike, she tore up one letter after another until finally she ran down the stairs and over to the church. "A good sign," her mother thought. But when the girl got there, she took the statue of the Blessed Mother, hid it under her cloak, and ran back to her room. Then she wrote her final letter: "Dear God, I got your mama. If you want to see her again, send the bike!"

We laugh at these stories, not simply because they are ridiculous, but because there is a grain of truth in them. Many Catholics prefer to go to Mary rather than directly to Jesus or the Father. Protestants see this as a detour that elevates Mary above God. As for the statue thief, she thought that if she kidnapped God's mother, God would *have* to act.

There are, admittedly, some Catholics whose Marian devotions give us the chills because they deviate from official Church teaching. But when we correctly understand Mary's role in God's plan of salvation, we see that far from her leading us away from Jesus, she makes him more real for us. I am reminded of the time I saw a bandana-coiffed Croatian woman in Medugorje holding the hand of a life-sized outdoor statue of Mary. She was talking to Mary as if to her next-door neighbor. When she finished her conversation, she released Mary's hand, turned to go, hesitated, and turned back, as if to say, "Oh, yes, and I forgot to tell you something else." Here was a woman who was, I'm sure, in intense contact with God but who felt more comfortable pouring out her heart to another woman. That woman was also the Mother of God, but her feminine humanity was inviting and readily accessible.

Revelation in History and in the Heart

God's revelation comes to us in two ways. There is what we can call his *objective* revelation, that is, the events, facts, and historical circumstances God used to reveal himself and his plan for the world. We read those things in the Bible. Even the existence of the Bible itself is one of those objective, historical acts of God revealing himself. The most dramatic and central act in this revelation was the death and resurrection of Jesus Christ. Jesus was crucified under Pontius Pilate. When Pilate washed his hands and let the soldiers drag the cross-bearing Nazarene to Calvary, little did he realize that he was anchoring in history an event in which he, the Roman procurator, would be remembered by name for the next two thousand years—in fact, every time Christians recite their creed.

But that objective side of revelation, that anchoring of revelation in history, would have been as useless as a bottled message bobbing in the ocean if there were not the *subjective* side of revelation, that is, revelation as it is received by human hearts. "'What eye has not seen, and ear has not heard, and what has not entered the human heart, what God has prepared for those who love him,' this God has revealed to us through the Spirit. . . . We have not received the spirit of the world but the Spirit that is from God, so that we may understand the things freely given us by God" (1 Corinthians 2:9-10, 12, NAB).

The Holy Spirit makes God's external revelation happen within us. That is what Jesus means when he speaks of the Holy Spirit as the revealer: "He will take from what is mine and declare it to you" (John 16:15, NAB). Of course, this supposes that we have the receptivity of faith. But once faith is there, the whole drama of salvation history is played out in our hearts. That internal revelation is the work of the Holy Spirit.

Several things should be noted about this interior revelation. First, although it is interior to the heart of every believer, it is common to the whole communion of believers. It is personal but not individualistic. Since it is one and the same Spirit who reveals, it is basically the same message for everyone, namely, the mystery of the triune God, which again gets externalized in the teaching of the Church—what we call "Tradition." That does not mean that every insight into revelation is given to everyone; the Fathers of the Church each brought their insights, and so have saints and mystics down through the ages. But as the authentic insights of individuals flow into the great river of Tradition, they enrich it and make it the heritage of all.

Second, since what the Holy Spirit is revealing is God himself, the mystery he reveals is limitless. But for the Holy Spirit, this is not a problem. "The Spirit explores everything, even the depths of God" (1 Corinthians 2:10). For seventy-five years, the Titanic lay hidden on the floor of the Atlantic Ocean until explorers dropped searchlights and cameras to its depths and revealed the treasure. That is what the Holy Spirit does for the depths of God. A tour guide taking you through Carlsbad Caverns in New Mexico will point out the stunning creations nature has formed over millions of years. So does the Holy Spirit for the stunning wonders of God. Imagine what it is like when the One you are exploring is God and your guide, your revealer, is none other than the Spirit of God!

Third, it follows that the Spirit's revelation is progressive. Even though we may not be as holy as the early Christians, we understand some things better than they did because the Holy Spirit has gradually unwrapped the mystery of Jesus over the centuries. This progression happens to us not merely as Church but personally, as we grow in our knowledge and understanding of God.

Fourth, the Holy Spirit uses the example of other people to move us interiorly to greater holiness, to greater conformity with Jesus. In explaining the parable of the sower, Jesus says that the seed is the "word" of God, a seed that he immediately begins to describe as "people": "The sower sows the word. These are the ones on the path. . . . And these are the ones sown on rocky ground. . . . Those sown among thorns . . . are . . . the people. . . . But those sown on rich soil are the ones . . ." (Mark 4:14-16, 18, 20, NAB).

Mary, Mold and Model

And who is the number one exemplar that the Spirit uses to inspire us? It is Jesus, of course. But Jesus cannot model response to Jesus. I remember a major television presentation by Fr. John Powell, a Jesuit professor at Loyola University in Chicago. It was a compelling lecture, but the camera spent one-third of the time focusing on the responses of the audience. One woman in the audience, perhaps the priest's sister, was so taken by his talk that you could read it in her eyes. She so caught me up in her enthusiasm that I began to say interiorly "Amen" after each of Fr. Powell's sentences. Similarly, there are countless others who have modeled for us how to follow Jesus, how to be conformed to him. From Francis I learn Jesus' poverty; from Ignatius, Jesus' obedience; from the great Teresa of Avila, Jesus' prayer; from Thérèse of Lisieux, Jesus' simplicity; from Augustine, Jesus' wisdom; from Thomas Aquinas, Jesus' love of the truth; from the martyrs, Jesus' fidelity to death.

All these are models, yet imperfect models. The perfect model? The one fashioned by the Holy Spirit to embody the perfect response to Jesus? MARY. But even before Jesus was the model for her or anyone else, she was the model for him. How so? She was the mold from which the Holy Spirit fashioned God in the flesh—God from the flesh of Mary! Jesus' physical traits must have resembled hers. But more important, God chose her and made her to be the mold, the model if you will, for his humanity. Her flesh was sinless, made so by the one to be born of her. And so the humanity of Jesus was sinless, not merely because he was God, but because he took sinless flesh from Mary. A metallurgist knows that any imperfection in the mold for a gold medal will show up in the finished product. The mold for Jesus was perfect. And so was the product, Jesus' perfectly holy humanity.

There is much more to explore in this foundational event we call the incarnation. In it Mary becomes the Mother of God, *Theotokos¸* "God-bearer," as the Greek fathers called her. The privilege is so unique that no one else can share it. But Mary's greatness is also—and even more important—measured by her role in her Son's mission, in the gathering of the elect. And for this she walks beside us as a pilgrim. For she, too, walks by faith and not by sight (2 Corinthians 5:7). And here, too, is the mystery that joins distance and closeness, the far and the near, transcendence and immanence. Before the Mother of God, we fall on our knees; with Mary the pilgrim we walk holding hands.

We can do that, of course, because Mary is not just any pilgrim. She is the ideal pilgrim, the one blessed because she believed (Luke 1:45), the one who in the darkness hoped against hope (Romans 4:18), the one who loved as no other loved.

....

Masterpiece of the Holy Spirit, mold for the humanity of God, perfect pilgrim, walk with us through the pages of this book that we may reach more quickly him whom your heart loves (Song of Songs 3:1-4). *Amen.*

FOR REFLECTION

1. In this meditation, what new insight struck you?

2. Have you ever tried looking at Jesus or one of the gospel scenes with the eyes of Mary?

3. Why are both external and internal revelation important?

Chapter 2

Overshadowed

Eduardo and his wife, Tanya, had been trying for months to conceive a child. Married in their thirties, they knew their biological clocks were ticking. Eduardo's first wife had died of cancer, leaving him with two young daughters. The older daughter, Ana, had been diagnosed with cancer when she was only ten months old and was still fighting the disease. And the younger daughter? At the age of nine, Maria had been killed when an eighteen-wheeler crushed Eduardo's BMW like tinfoil. The crash also killed Eduardo's friend, my niece Regina, whom he was thinking of marrying. Emerging from the trashed BMW with a broken arm and a heart more crushed than the car, Eduardo struggled for months to cope with this series of unexplainable tragedies. Death, it seemed, was hounding him at every turn.

But with Tanya a new life began, and they ardently hoped that soon they would hold a baby in their arms. Yet the months dragged on with no sign of new life. Finally they came to me asking that I pray over them for the gift of fertility. That I did, invoking Mary and her cousin, Elizabeth, both of whom conceived when nature said they couldn't. I also invoked the Holy Spirit, who had worked the miracle of Mary's conception of Jesus. As we prayed, Tanya had a vision of Mary and Elizabeth that consoled her; yet at the same time, she was troubled by the vision because she felt overwhelmed by her own unworthiness in the presence of these holy women. "How could someone like me win God's approval enough to be heard?" Tanya thought. Gradually the Lord healed Tanya of this self-rejection, and then she heard the doctor say, "Tanya, you're pregnant!" She gave birth to a whopping baby boy, who at eight-and-a-half pounds had to be delivered by Caesarean section.

I don't know what kind of switchboard communication went on in heaven as a result of our prayer, but certainly God gave the answer—with the bonus of a spiritual healing in the process of blessing new life in Tanya's womb.

The Bible, too, has stories like Tanya and Eduardo's. Elkanah's wife, Hannah, was childless in a culture that shamed sterility. Elkanah's other wife, blessed with children, needled her with ridicule. But Hannah poured out her affliction before the Lord at Shiloh, and three years later she offered at the shrine her weaned child, Samuel, who became the prophet-anointer of Israel's first kings (1 Samuel 1:28). Abraham's wife, Sarah, had also been unable to conceive, despite the Lord's repeated promise that Abraham would have a legitimate son. The Lord delayed the promise until Sarah was too old to conceive—by human standards. But Abraham, "hoping against hope" (Romans 4:18), continued to believe. One day, to his surprise, three strangers showed up at his tent at midday. True to the laws of hospitality and even more diligent in carrying them out, Abraham called himself their servant, ran to greet them, washed their feet, slaughtered a calf, and presented them with a feast. In reply, one of them said, "I will surely return to you about this time next year, and Sarah will then have a son" (Genesis 18:10, NAB). When Sarah laughed in disbelief, the visitor said, "Is anything too marvelous for the LORD to do?" (18:14, NAB). For indeed it was the Lord who had appeared to Abraham in the person of the three strangers (18:1-2). Sarah soon conceived and gave birth to Isaac.

Finally, there was Manoah's wife, to whom an angel appeared in human form and said, "Though you are barren and have had no children, yet you will conceive and bear a son" (Judges 13:3, NAB). That son was Samson, the "superman" of the period of the judges. Manoah offered a sacrifice "to the LORD, whose works are mysteries" (13:19, NAB).

Daughter Zion

Mysteries, yes, but none so great as what happened in an obscure village of Galilee when, in answer to centuries of prayer for a messiah, the divine messenger spoke to a young girl: "Hail, most highly favored one. The Lord is with you" (Luke 1:28). Who was this maid? "The virgin's name was Mary," betrothed to a man named Joseph (1:27). What surprised her was not, according to the text, the appearance of an angel but the greeting. She must have thought:

What is so special about me, that I should be hailed this way, so highly favored? And why did he not address me with the normal Jewish greeting—"Peace"? Instead he said, "Rejoice!" [the real meaning of the word most often translated "Hail"]. That sounded a lot like the prophets trumpeting the dawn of salvation, as in Zephaniah: "Rejoice, O daughter Zion, / sing joyfully, O Israel! / Be glad and exult with all your heart, / O daughter Jerusalem! . . . / The LORD, your God, is in your midst, a mighty savior" [3:14, 17].

In fact, whether or not Mary realized it at that moment, she was daughter Zion, daughter Jerusalem, told to rejoice at the coming of the Savior (the meaning of Jesus' name) in her midst—in her womb.

"Fear not, Mary," the angel reassured her, using again the same language in Zephaniah (3:16). "You have found favor with God. You will conceive in your womb and bear a son, and you will call his name Jesus. He will be great and will be called Son of the Most High. And the Lord God will give him the throne of David, his father. And he will reign over the house of Jacob forever, and of his kingdom there will be no end" (Luke 1:30-33).

If Mary was overwhelmed with the greeting, she must have been even more overwhelmed by this description of the mission given to her. Did she understand the enormous scope of the message? Probably not. First of all, how could this be, since in the puzzling account of Luke, though engaged she had resolved to remain a virgin? But then, what did it mean that her son, the Messiah, would reign over the house of Jacob *forever*?

The angel explained that this would be no ordinary birth. "The holy Spirit will come upon you, and the power of the Most High will overshadow you. Therefore the child to be born will be called holy, the Son of God" (Luke 1:35, NAB). In the Hebrew Scriptures, which Mary knew, the Spirit of God often came upon those anointed for a mission, like the heroes in the Book of Judges and the prophets and kings Saul and David. But whoever heard of the Holy Spirit coming, without human help, to work the conception of a child in a virginal womb? The angel's explanation of the manner in which the conception would take place must have been even more puzzling to Mary than the call to be the mother of the Messiah.

Ark of the Covenant

The angel said that the Holy Spirit, the power of the Most High, would *overshadow* her. That would have reminded her of the cloud overshadowing the ark of the covenant. The cloud revealed God's presence in a visible way, confirming that the tablets of the law resting in the ark were indeed his word. He had pitched his tent in the midst of his people, and his word was etched in stone. But the Word of God in Mary would be flesh etched of her flesh, God in person.

As much as the people of Israel rejoiced to have the Lord in their midst, they nevertheless trembled with fear and awe before the ark. Only Moses was allowed to enter the tent housing the ark. And later, when the ark was in the temple in Jerusalem, only the high priest was allowed to enter once a year. If the Israelites approached the dwelling with such fear and awe, what is to be said of us, the people of the new covenant, before the ark that housed the Son of God in the flesh!

The achievement of this marvel was the work of the Holy Spirit.

St. Luke leaves to our imagination and to the Church's reflection what this unique union of Mary with the Holy Spirit meant for her. Of one thing we can be sure: God did not use Mary as a mere physical instrument for the conception of Jesus. Just as he allowed her mind to question, he also sought the free consent of her will. St. Bernard pictures the whole unredeemed world holding its breath, pleading for Mary to say yes to this call. Once it was clear to her that this was what God wanted, she wanted it too. "Let it be done to me as you have said" (Luke 1:38). Both her mind and her will were fully engaged.

"Engaged" is a good word, for it is also used for the mutual commitment of couples who intend to marry. But in this case, there was no delay from engagement to marriage, nor was there a delay in achieving the goal of the union, the conception of Jesus. There was no mutual vow made of "Till death do us part"; the union would last for eternity. In this mutual commitment and cooperation, the Church's tradition has endowed Mary with the title "Spouse of the Holy Spirit." Because of the way God does things, with perfect respect for the person he engages in a mission, Mary does not cease being the spouse of the Holy Spirit after Jesus is born any more than parents cease to be married once their child is born. In Mary's case, because she lives now in heavenly glory, her spousal relation with the Holy Spirit is a living, eternally enduring reality.

Because the Holy Spirit's union with Mary is a spiritual one, taking place within her body and spirit, wherever Mary is, the Holy Spirit is. There has never been a divorce. If Paul could say of every Christian, "Your body is a temple of the holy Spirit" (1 Corinthians 6:19, NAB), then this is true of Mary in an eminent way. If we are to glorify God in our bodies (6:20), then Mary certainly glorifies God in hers, making visible the presence and the action of the Holy Spirit. That is why the authentic apparitions of Mary are really apparitions of the Holy Spirit working through her, as we will consider in another chapter. But for now, let us return to Nazareth and see what the Holy Spirit is inspiring Mary to do next.

....

Lord, if I am overwhelmed by the vast mysteries of the universe that are revealed by sophisticated telescopes, how much more am I awed by the work of your Holy Spirit in the womb of

Mary. What dignity you have given our human nature by joining yourself to it and taking us up into the life of the Trinity! May I share Mary's awe of this mystery, and may I have her joyful surrender to your call in my life. Amen.

FOR REFLECTION

1. Can you recall a moment in your life when you were surprised by God?

2. Have you ever felt God was calling you to do something beyond your own power? How could the scene of Mary at the annunciation help you?

3. What does the image of Mary as the ark of the covenant suggest to you?

Chapter 3

Sent

It was my month to be bell ringer. In the novitiate's morning, that meant opening the window halfway up in one building and ringing the hand bell loud enough so that it could be heard in the dormitory next door. There was another bell on the property, an old railroad bell that was now serving to announce three o'clock prayer and the end of the afternoon work period. It was loud enough not only to call the novices from work in the outlying field but also to awaken anyone who happened to be napping in the nearby town of Galesville. Novice that I was in matters of audiology, it never occurred to me that such was the reason the old railroad bell was never rung early in the morning or late at night.

It so happened that one morning, as I went to the window to perform my appointed duty, a laymen's retreat was beginning in a third building. Harold, a fellow novice, stopped me with this urgent message: "Father Novice Master told me to tell you to ring the bell outside this morning." This was obviously to awaken the retreatants as well. Obediently I retraced my steps and approached the railroad bell, which was indeed outside. I had my hand on the rope when the frame of the novice master suddenly loomed behind me: "I said to ring the bell *outside*, not the *outside bell!*"

It was neither the first nor the last time in my life that I hadn't listened well enough. Fortunately for all of us, Mary listened well. She heard the whole message. Had I been the newly installed

29

Mother of God, I would probably have sat down and waited for the processions to begin. But Mary heard more than her call to be God's First Lady. Her cousin Elizabeth was in need. Mary heard that. The angel hadn't told her to go to Elizabeth's aid—but the Holy Spirit did. Mary had proclaimed herself servant of the Lord. Now she would be the servant of Elizabeth.

There is something truly striking about this sequence. Mary teams up with the Holy Spirit to bring God to earth. Then the Spirit immediately sends her on a mission. Mary *goes*, and she goes *"with haste"* (Luke 1:39). The Greek word *spoudē* can also mean "eagerness," "diligence," even "zeal." Luke is preparing us for the Pentecost of the Church by giving us a cameo Pentecost right here. Filled with the Spirit, Mary hastens to share the good news, and she does so by meeting someone else's need. And so it will happen at the public Pentecost: The Holy Spirit births the Church and sends forth its members as if he were blowing on a cluster of dandelion seeds. But there is a difference. In the Acts of the Apostles, the Holy Spirit sets off a nuclear fireball. With Mary and Elizabeth, he lights two intimate candles, the flame of the one lighting the other—a domestic Pentecost.

Why is this significant? Because most of us are not called to be missionaries to the world in the way the apostles were. But we are called to live out a domestic Pentecost. Our mission is right where we are, within our families, in our workplaces, in our communities. Yes, he calls us to be missionaries. Better said, if we have received the Holy Spirit, he will *move* us to be missionaries. He will put in our hearts *spoudē,* the eagerness and the zeal that moved Mary and later Paul, who said, "The love of Christ impels us" (2 Corinthians 5:14, NAB). But don't dream of evangelizing foreign lands if you are not evangelizing the ground on which you stand.

Mary Moves South

So carrying Jesus and filled with the Spirit, Mary moves south, reaching the hill country of Judea. This detail is not lost on the Church as it contemplates this scene in her liturgy: "Hark! My lover—here he comes / springing across the mountains, / leaping across the hills" (Song of Songs 2:8, NAB). Mary was walking, or at best riding on a donkey, but her heart was like a deer, flying over rocks and ravines with great news. Tradition has it that she arrived at the village of Ein Karem (Vineyard Spring), a fitting setting for the creator of all life whom Mary was carrying in her womb. There "she entered the house of Zechariah" (Luke 1:40, NAB). Zechariah, like Mary, had been visited by a heavenly messenger announcing the birth of a son, John the Baptist. But unlike Mary, he had doubted that such an event was possible to a couple as aged as he and his wife were. The event literally left him speechless—not from wonder, but from his feeble faith. So it is not surprising that he has nothing to say and makes no appearance when Mary greets Elizabeth. In Luke's story, the women steal the show.

When Elizabeth heard Mary's greeting, the infant leaped in her womb, and Elizabeth, filled with the holy Spirit, cried out in a loud voice and said, "Most blessed are you among women, and blessed is the fruit of your womb. And how does this happen to me, that the mother of my Lord should come to me? For at the moment your greeting reached my ears, the infant in my womb leaped for joy." (Luke 1:41-44, NAB)

Elizabeth must have been in the back of the house, for it is not the sight of Mary that launches their interaction but the sound of her voice. That detail is significant for more than one reason. From now on, the living voice will be the privileged way of sharing the good news. (At Mass, missalettes let us *see* the word, but the Church wants us to *listen* to it.) The baby John could not see Mary, but he could hear her. "Faith comes by hearing" (Romans 10:17). It is at the sound of Mary's voice that the Holy Spirit acts, thus confirming the intimate and ongoing relation of Mary with the Holy Spirit. All Mary has to do is to sing out, "Shalom, Elizabeth!" and the Holy Spirit leaps to her cousin and makes the unborn dance. David danced before the ark (2 Samuel 6:14), but he was an adult. John dances even before he walks.

The Holy Spirit does more than excite mother and child. Elizabeth obviously receives a word of knowledge from the Spirit informing her that Mary, too, is pregnant. And more than that, she is "the mother of my Lord" (Luke 1:43). Just as the whole of Luke's infancy gospel is a domestic Pentecost, so this scene is already suffused with the light of Easter and the confession that Jesus is Lord. Elizabeth manifests the Holy Spirit within her by this confession, for as Paul will say, "No one can say, 'Jesus is Lord,' except by the holy Spirit" (1 Corinthians 12:3, NAB). Elizabeth finds on her lips the words of David— "How can the ark of the LORD come to me?" (2 Samuel 6:9, NAB)—when she says, "How does this happen to me, that the mother of my Lord should come to me?" (Luke 1:44, NAB).

Here, then, is another way in which Luke is hinting that Mary is the new ark of the covenant.

Elizabeth concludes: "Blessed are you who believed that what was spoken to you by the Lord would be fulfilled" (Luke 1:45, NAB). This is Elizabeth's second blessing of Mary. In the first, she blessed her for being "mother of my Lord." Now she blesses Mary for her faith. The older woman may have been thinking of Zechariah's disbelief, but the fact is that Mary, too, had to believe that what the angel had promised her would be fulfilled. After all, there was no immediate physical confirmation of her pregnancy. But Mary did act upon the revelation that her cousin was pregnant and would soon need help. And indeed she found it to be so when the two expectant mothers met.

And so we encounter a thread that will appear again in the gospels: Faith in Jesus is more important than blood relations. In fact, Jesus' blood is going to fashion a new family. Mary's blessedness is greater because she believed than because she conceived. When a woman in the crowd cries out, "Blessed is the womb that bore you and the breasts that nursed you!" Jesus replies, "Blessed, rather, are those who hear the word of God and obey it" (Luke 11:27, 28). Far from putting down his mother, Jesus is proclaiming her superior blessing because she believed, a blessing in which everyone who believes can share. And yet we must also say that if Jesus' blood shed on the cross created a new family, then that blood was originally taken from Mary.

In Mary's hymn of praise, all generations will join in calling her blessed. To that we turn in the next chapter.

....

Lord, grant me a listening ear like that of Mary, who heard and acted on everything you said. Even when I hear your word or read it, I rarely hear everything you have to tell me. You want me to ponder the great things you have done for me, but you also call me to act. Cleanse the ears of my heart. Fill me with your Holy Spirit, and empower me to share your great news with others in my family, among my friends, and at my workplace. May the Holy Spirit whom you have given to me bless those I meet, and may that same Spirit echo back a blessing for me as well. Amen.

FOR REFLECTION

1. Mary was a perfect listener. How do you evaluate your own listening ability?

2. Mary was servant to the Lord and to her extended family. How do you see this to be a double call in your own life?

3. What would it be like for your family to experience a domestic Pentecost? How can this happen?

Chapter 4

Praise

Our earth is pockmarked with craters that are occasionally wakened by the tremendous heat and pressure underground. When a crater bursts to the sky, we call it a volcano eruption. When the Holy Spirit enters deeply into a person, the urge to praise is almost irresistible. I say "almost" because the Holy Spirit never forces our free will. But ordinarily, the experience is so wonderful that no one wants to resist. Thus I dare to liken it to the eruption of a volcano, with the only caveat being that it is not destructive or disorderly but gloriously life-giving.

So it happened at Pentecost when the mighty wind blew into the upper room and changed a crowd of fearful Jews into a chorus of disciples so overcome with joyful praise that some thought they were drunk. With Mary, according to Luke's narrative, the pressure to turn her blessing to praise exploded in the Magnificat, a beautiful, orderly hymn glorifying the Lord (1:46-55). As she burst into praise, she foreshadowed the universal Pentecostal praise of the early community in Acts 2. She did in person what the Church would do as a community.

There is no need to insist that the Magnificat is the work of the Holy Spirit. When later, Zechariah, with tongue loosed, bursts into his hymn of blessing at the birth of his son, John, Luke says he was prophesying; that is, he was moved by the Holy Spirit

(1:67). Luke has already portrayed Mary as being led by the Spirit, so when she bursts forth in praise and thanksgiving, he does not repeat this statement.

Where does Mary get the words for her song? Of course, from the Holy Spirit, but she naturally picks up the language of the Old Testament, which was probably the sum of her vocabulary. Luke says that Mary "kept all these things," pondering them in her heart (2:19; see also 2:51). "Pondering" translates a Greek word that also means "comparing," and it suggests that she was thinking of what her present experience meant in the light of the events in the history of her people. In the present case, it was not difficult to find a previous event like Mary's that called forth a song of praise— Hannah's song at the birth of Samuel (1 Samuel 2:1-10).

Though there are significant differences in the two songs, the common thread is the triumph of the "see-saw" God, raising the lowly and casting down the proud. Like Hannah, Mary wraps her personal thanks into the larger praise and thanks of her people. Far from seeing her inestimable privilege of being mother of the Son of God as separating her from her people, Mary proclaims her honor as being typical of God's action in the story of Israel, a fulfillment of what he had done and promised long ago. In this way, Mary deflects attention from herself and hails the enfleshment of the Messiah as the glory of her people.

This melting of the individual into the collective was a common trait in the culture of biblical times. Modern scholars have called it the "dyadic personality," the tendency to think first in terms of the group and only second in terms of the individual. Even today this same cultural trait exists in the tribes of Africa and India, as I was able to observe firsthand during my six years in Nepal and India. Mary is a typical Jewish woman of her times, and thus she automatically thinks of what the incarnation means for her people. But she also shows great humility in giving all the glory to God.

Threads of the Old Testament

If the song of Hannah was the template for Mary's song, then the expressions she uses are really threads of many Old Testament texts woven skillfully into a beautiful tapestry. My Greek New Testament lists thirty-five cross-references for the Magnificat alone. Those of us who have little acquaintance with the Old Testament would not be able to appreciate how the verses of Mary's song would have reverberated in the hearts of the Jewish Christians. Everything would have been familiar, a little like the familiarity we have with our national anthem. But it would also have been a new song, celebrating the wedding of the old and the new.

"My soul glorifies the Lord," she begins, *"and my spirit rejoices in God my savior"* (Luke 1:46, 47). Notice the connection of praise with joy. Like Mary, when the Holy Spirit moves us to praise God, our spirit is filled with joy, which Paul lists as the first fruit of the Spirit after love (Galatians 5:22). Although the Holy Spirit often moves us to praise spontaneously—"volcanically," if you wish—it is also true that there are times when we don't feel like praising and we don't feel the joy that comes with it. These are times when we are challenged to offer "the sacrifice of praise" (Psalm 50:23), to begin praising God simply because we know he is worthy of praise, whether we feel like it or not. If we continue doing so, the gift of joy will return. A friend of mine has found

that praising God enables her to overcome her chronic bouts of depression. For her, praise works better than pills.

Mary also calls God her savior. She needed redemption as much as anyone else, but the Holy Spirit has led the Church to understand that in view of the future merits of her son, his mother was preserved from original sin from the moment of her conception. The timing made the difference—before Jesus' death and resurrection rather than (like the rest of us) after it. But she could still call her son her savior.

"For he has looked on the lowliness of his servant" (Luke 1:48). For God to "look" upon someone is to lift them up. Jesus would later say, "He who humbles himself will be exalted" (Luke 14:11; 18:14). Mary calls herself nothing more than the servant of the Lord, just as she did at the annunciation (1:38). And yet this servant will be called "blessed" by all generations. To be "blessed" means to be the recipient of a gift, and Mary proclaims that all she has and is comes as God's gift, not as something that she has merited. World-renowned Pentecostal leader David du Plessis, who is called "Mister Pentecost," once said, "I want to be part of those generations that call Mary blessed." In every Hail Mary, we join Elizabeth and those generations when we say, "Blessed art thou among women, and blessed is the fruit of thy womb, Jesus."

"The Mighty One has done great things for me" (Luke 1:49). We do not become more humble by minimizing the gifts that God has given us. Mary didn't. To do so would be to claim those gifts as something we produced or merited. If they are God's gifts, then it is not pride to say how wonderful they are, for they are God's doing, not ours. In the movie *Chariots of Fire*, one of the champion runners says, "When I run, I feel His pleasure."

It's important, of course, that we don't claim gifts that we don't have, or greater gifts than we have been given. I know a lady in one parish who cannot carry a tune, but she sings so loudly and boldly that a man in the next pew, who sings well, sings beyond his normal volume in order to drown her out.

"Holy is his name" (Luke 1:49). This, too, comes from the Holy Spirit's inspiration of Mary. It echoes Psalm 111:9: "Holy and awesome is your name." It will become part of the prayer Jesus teaches when he says, "Hallowed be thy name" (Matthew 6:9). The common understanding is that God's name is sacred and that we should accordingly worship it, reverence it, and in the Lord's Prayer, ask that the whole world come to know and worship the Father.

But if we listen to Ezekiel 36:20-32, we hear that the Lord shows his name to be holy by his saving intervention on behalf of his people: "I will prove the holiness of my great name. . . . I will give you a new heart and place a new spirit within you, taking from your bodies your stony hearts and giving you hearts of flesh. I will put my spirit within you" (36:23, 26). In other words, when Mary says God's name is holy, she means what the Old Testament means: Our God is an acting God, a saving God, a God who breaks into history and does mighty deeds. In fact, that is just what Mary proclaimed in the preceding line: "The Mighty One has done great things for me." And that power of the name, the power of the Holy Spirit, is always there, like a rocket waiting to be launched. When Mary sings that God's name is holy, she is praising not just how God has shown the dynamic power of his name in working the miraculous conception. She is also saying what a father might say to his children as he lights a firecracker on the Fourth of July: "Look out—something wonderful is going to happen!"

In the next verses, Mary becomes truly prophetic. She tells what the mystery of her call and gift means for her people and for the world: *"His mercy is for generations and generations. / He has shown the might of his arm. / He has scattered the proud in the conceit of their heart. / He has cast down rulers from their thrones / and lifted up the lowly. / He has filled the hungry with good things, / and the rich he has sent away empty"* (Luke 1:50-53). Although God's action is described here as past, this is what is called the "prophetic perfect"; that is, although this is what God *will* do, it has already been determined in what he *has* done. The incarnation—which is the work of the Holy Spirit and Mary—is turning the world's values upside down. It launches a program for changing the world. All of this because of what's taking place in a tiny cell growing in the womb of Mary. Mary not only believes that she has conceived, but she also believes in the future that is coming because of it. Her faith is also hope—biblical hope, which is not wishful thinking but assurance because God has promised it.

God's Faithfulness to His Promises

And that is what she says in the concluding lines: *"He has helped Israel, his servant, remembering his mercy (as he promised our fathers) to Abraham and his descendants forever"* (Luke 1:54-55). God's love for his people Israel, shown in the past and now brought to a climax in the sending of the Savior, means that he has remembered Abraham. This puts the coming of the Holy

Spirit upon Mary, the conception of Jesus, and all that follows in the framework of an intimate friendship. When we remember someone's birthday by calling them or sending them a card, we strengthen a bond of friendship and love. When God remembers, he does more; he moves to save. So God "remembered" Noah floating on the flood waters and sent a wind to dry them up (Genesis 8:1). God "remembered" Abraham and saved his nephew Lot (19:29). God "remembered" Rachel and enabled her to conceive (30:22). He "remembered" his covenant with Abraham and sent Moses to lead his people to freedom (Exodus 2:24). So God has now remembered his mercy and his loving kindness to Abraham and has sent his offspring, Jesus, to save his people.

To non-Jews—and that is most of us—it may sound odd that sending Jesus is God's remembering an ancestor lost in the mist of remote times. But the Jews had a keen sense of God's fidelity, his faithfulness to his promises. Jesus is not just a savior suddenly sent to rescue a world gone amok; he is the fulfillment of a promise. This is a major theme of Paul's Letter to the Romans. God has fulfilled his promise—has shown himself righteous to his covenant promise—by sending Jesus.

Thus, Mary's mention of Abraham at the finale of her song is significant. She sees her blessing not just in cosmic hues for the future; she sees it as climaxing a love story that had begun thousands of years earlier when God chose Abraham and made him the father of nations (Genesis 17:4-6). Moreover, God blessed Abraham because of his faith in God's incredible promise (15:6). Mary, too, unlike Zechariah but in perfect sync with father Abraham, is blessed for her faith in an even more incredible promise (Luke 1:45).

It was the Holy Spirit who inspired Mary's hymn of praise. The same Holy Spirit wants to inspire ours.

....

Father, in choosing Mary to be the mother of your Son, you filled her with the Holy Spirit, gave her the power to praise you beyond human strength, and inspired her in her Magnificat to be the first interpreter of the mystery of the incarnation. Fill me with the Spirit of praise so that I may always bless you for your gift, be bold to share my joy, and in Mary's company continue to treasure and ponder the wonderful things that you have done in the history of your people and in me. Amen.

FOR REFLECTION

1. What place does praise have in your life?

2. The Holy Spirit inspires praise and prays within us in ways that go beyond speech. Do you ask the Holy Spirit to move me with his gift of praise?

3. Do you praise God for the gifts he has bestowed on others?

Chapter 5

Pondering

The Holy Spirit is a river. Jesus says the water he gives is "living water" (John 4:10) that flows as rivers flow (7:37-39). At the end of the Book of Revelation, the prophet sees in heaven the river of life-giving water flowing from the throne of God and the Lamb (22:1), an image of the Holy Spirit who proceeds from the Father and the Son.

My first experience of a river was the one I swam in as a kid—the Medina—which ran for a mile and a half at the edge of our family's ranch. On either side of this flowing green ribbon stood huge cypress sentinels, whose limbs reached out to each other, forming the nave of a natural Gothic cathedral. The river had a personality of its own. Sometimes it chattered gleefully as it met the rapids. At other times it guarded a deep silence, reflecting the ten-foot-deep bed over which it seemed hardly to move.

So it is with the river of the Spirit. So it is as the Spirit that led Mary to explode with praise in the Magnificat now shows us the pregnant woman in silence, letting events unfold as the Lord has planned, and contemplating the depths of what is transpiring. The Spirit now is like still waters, fresh and full of life but quiet and deep. No words of Mary are recorded until she finds Jesus at the age of twelve in the temple. In the meantime, what were her thoughts? I asked a young mother who had recently given birth what kind of thoughts went through her mind during her pregnancy. This is what she wrote:

I felt total joy at discovering I was pregnant. I was amazed and felt touched by God. To see the baby on the sonogram was so incredible—he looked like a tiny circle that pulsates. It was like each heartbeat praised God, sang for joy, announced new life! I wanted to watch and listen forever. I began to wonder what he would look like—his smile, his eyes. Would he be an engineer like his father? Artistic? Athletic? Maybe a priest? Would he resemble my husband or me or both of us? I began to talk to him.

Other pregnant women read about pregnancy. I wanted to read about God. Daily I prayed for him to be healthy, for Mary to be with me in carrying the baby, for Jesus to protect the baby in the womb, for the baby to know our joy in receiving this gift of his life. I wondered how Mary prepared for the birth of Jesus. I prepared for our baby's arrival by taking on the house. I did projects that were on our "to-do" list for a long time—walls painted, rooms rearranged. I loved being pregnant even though during the last three months, it was more physically difficult.

Mary's thoughts and feelings must have been similar in many ways, although she did not have the chance to see her baby in a sonogram or hear his heartbeat with a stethoscope. But the Lord had given her plenty to think about, especially about her baby's future:

What did the angel mean: "He will be great"? Does that mean he will be a rabbi or a prophet? "Son of the Most High," he said. That's more than a rabbi or prophet. That means Son of God. And he will sit on David's throne. We have not had a king in David's line for five hundred years. Will there be a revolution? Will he throw out the Romans? What about the priests in the temple who have been running the show since we got back from the exile? They seem to have gotten very entrenched in the temple. They would likely be threatened by anyone who claimed to be the Messiah. Will Jesus take over their power?

And what could it mean that my son will reign over the house of Jacob forever . . . and that his kingdom will last forever? How can he reign forever when Scripture says that every man is mortal? Well, at least I know one thing: Isaiah said that the virgin would conceive and bear a son. It looks like that has been fulfilled in me, although I don't understand it all. And it's not been easy with the neighbors, seeing that I am pregnant and Joseph came late on the scene. But thank God for Joseph. He stood up for me and in front of the village said, "This woman is my wife, and the child is mine."

During those months, surely Mary pondered the Scriptures to find out what the Messiah would be like and what it would mean to be his mother. Maybe Joseph pointed out to her that every time a new king sat on the throne of David, the king's mother was mentioned. Or that the king's mother was known as "the Great Lady," who took the place of the queen in the Davidic dynasty, who had a throne next to her son with the right to intercede with him for the needy in the kingdom. And all of these ideas about royalty flooding her mind while she was cleaning the table and washing the dishes in a backward village in Galilee. It seemed so incredible! Yet even this pondering was part of the Holy Spirit's work in her, for he was teaching her how to live without knowing all the answers, to live by faith and not by sight (2 Corinthians 5:7). In the midst of that night journey, she had no clue that future millions would look to her as they struggled with unanswered questions, even about God—such as the parent whose child would die at the age of two, the bride-to-be whose fiancé would be killed in battle, the woman whose husband would abandon her and their six children. (These are the stories of three women I have known.)

Where God Wanted Them

The journey to Bethlehem gave her more time to ponder. Arriving there, she and Joseph found the town anything but quiet, and there was "no room for them in the inn" (Luke 2:7, NAB). What does it feel like to have no suitable place to lodge for the night? One October in Nepal, we were taking the novices on our annual trek through the foothills of the Himalayas. A three-day walk from the nearest town, we reached the trekkers' lodge, euphemistically called a "hotel," only to find that every inch of the facility was taken. Apologizing, the owner said that the only space available was in the chicken shed, so that's where we slept. The chickens seemed upset at this intrusion, but finally guests and hosts slept peacefully, if not comfortably, together.

But this was nothing like the frustrating search for a birthing couch for Mary. Finally a trough with ox's straw became available, providing a bed for this child who the angel said was a king. Could straw be so welcoming? With two of my novices, I once visited a remote village in Nepal, where we were welcomed by a poor family that had no other place for us to lodge than on the floor of a storage room. The father covered the floor with armfuls of straw, and there we bedded down for the night. Strangely, I was flooded with love and joy as I fell asleep. If the Fathers of the Church could say that the Jordan waters were blessed by Jesus when he was baptized, I wondered if maybe the child Jesus hadn't blessed the straw we were sleeping on that night. The joy was in knowing that I was exactly where God wanted me to be.

If the Holy Spirit was with Mary and Joseph, I'm sure their joy that night was not only in the birth of Jesus but also in knowing that there, among the straw and the animals, was exactly where God wanted them to be. Did they fret because they didn't have better quarters? I think, rather, that they were beginning to understand what this God was about. He was a God who turns things upside down, a God who so loves the poor that he wanted to be born among them—or better yet, maybe even to take the place of a service animal for the night. After all, that's why he had come, to be a servant, like his mother. Showered with the joy of being right where God wanted them to be, in the home of service animals, Joseph and Mary might even have laughed at the ridiculous, topsy-turvy ways of the God who had caught them up in his Ferris wheel and was giving them the supernatural joy of the Holy Spirit (Galatians 5:22). (It was right here in this nativity scene that St. Francis the *Poverello* found the source of his joy, and it led him to people Italy with cribs for the Christ child.)

In the middle of the night, a handful of scraggly shepherds peered through the dark of the cave, their olive-skinned faces barely lit by the tiny oil lamp that Joseph was holding to greet them. Focusing on the baby, they beamed with joy as they spilled out a wonderful story of an angel telling them a savior had been born in Bethlehem, "who is Messiah and Lord" (Luke 2:11). The shepherds said they had heard a whole host of angels singing, "Glory to God in the highest, and peace to those whom he loves" (2:14). The world might think a manger bed the worst spot on earth for a newborn baby, and passing royalty might even scorn as trash the family that could provide nothing better than a manure-smelling home for him, but the shepherds and the heavenly hosts were seeing an incense-scented throne. And Mary, the bride of the Spirit, must have seen that as well, though it didn't change her physical discomfort or the barnyard smell.

In all of this, the gospel tells us nothing that she said, only that she pondered. In so doing, she is inviting us to contemplative awe before the mystery of the infinite God-become-flesh. If words seem so inadequate when we gaze on the mile-deep Grand Canyon or the thundering Niagara Falls, what is to be said before the mystery to which Mary has given birth? Nothing is to be said. Let your jaw drop. The Spirit-river is flowing deep—and in silence.

....

Holy Spirit, take my life with all its unanswered questions, and empower me as you did Mary to walk by faith rather than by sight. Help me to know that you are there even in the most unexpected circumstances, especially in the painful ones. Show me how all of this is part of the Father's work, fashioning me to be more like Jesus and training me for your service. Give me the courage to offer you some time daily to be my deep, still river so that I may see the events of my life as you see them, as part of the ongoing mystery that began with Mary's pondering and continues with me. Amen.

FOR REFLECTION

1. How does your experience of the Holy Spirit resemble a river?

2. Recall and perhaps share a time in your life when you had to walk by faith rather than by understanding. How was Mary's faith journey similar to your own experience?

3. Have you ever had a "no-room-at-the-inn" experience when you suddenly had to do without something you were expecting? How did you react? How might the Holy Spirit help you with a similar situation in the future?

Chapter 6

Surrender

Not only did the Word become flesh, he also became a Jew. Eight days after Jesus was born, Mary handed him to Joseph, who presented him to a local rabbi to be circumcised: the first shedding of Jesus' blood (Luke 2:21). When Jesus cried as his flesh was cut, Mary must have winced at his pain. But at this point, she may well have assumed that Jesus would grow up like any male Jew and that any more shedding of his blood would happen only by accident. If he were to be Messiah and Lord by God's decree, then he would not die a violent death. After all, he was to reign as king forever. It was not yet time for the Holy Spirit to unveil Jesus' more somber future to Mary. But that would soon come.

Jewish law required that a mother whose firstborn was a boy go to the temple after forty days for a rite of purification and offer either a lamb or two young pigeons or turtledoves. This ritual also provided the occasion for the Holy Family to *present* Jesus to the Lord, as Hannah had done with her child, Samuel. Mary and Joseph would not leave Jesus there, as Hannah had done with Samuel, because as Son of David and Messiah, he had another mission. Since Jesus was the firstborn, another Jewish law came into play, that of the redemption of the firstborn. In remembrance of the sparing of Israel's firstborn in the last plague on Egypt, every firstborn was understood to belong to the Lord but could be "bought back," or redeemed, by the paying of five shekels. Luke does not mention the five shekels, as he has combined this story with the purification, mentioning only the sacrifice of the doves. At any rate, there are two motifs here: the purification of Mary and the consecration and redemption of the firstborn.

What was the Holy Spirit doing in Mary as these early Jewish rituals were happening? This is all speculation, of course, because St. Luke gives us no clue as to what she was thinking. She remains silent, pondering. Certainly the Spirit was perfecting her obedience to the law. But the offering of Jesus, the presentation of him to the Lord, was the first external act by which Mary surrendered her son back to God. This was surely the grace of the Holy Spirit, for a mother's attachment to her child is the strongest of human ties. And in Mary's case, Jesus had been conceived in her womb by the power of the Holy Spirit and not by any man, so Jesus was hers in a way that no other son was his mother's. He was *totus tuus,* "totally yours." She knew, of course, that she and Joseph would receive him back at the end of the ritual. But the Holy Spirit was already schooling her in the joy of giving back to God, of saying "totally yours" to God, as God had made himself totally hers at conception. There is a Spanish song that hails "the sweet and total renunciation" that happens in the gift of self in committed love. Mary experiences that for the first time here as she releases Jesus to the Father.

However, the major focus of this temple scene is what happens next (Luke 2:22-38). The circumcision of the child was customary ritual; the approach of two elderly people was a surprise. The Holy Spirit had been at work in these elderly persons, both of whom represent Israel's hope for the Messiah. Three times Luke mentions the Holy Spirit in relation to Simeon. The Holy Spirit "was upon him" (2:25), the Holy Spirit had promised him that he would not die until he had seen the Messiah (2:26), and the Holy Spirit moved him to go to the temple precisely at the hour that the Holy Family was there and led him to them with a prophetic message (2:27). Again, Mary has the gift of ears. If anyone could embody the best of expectant Israel, it was Simeon. And he does not call Jesus the Messiah; he says more: "My eyes have seen your *salvation*" (2:30). Already this is the name given to him at the annunciation ("Jesus" means "God saves") and confirmed by the angel to the shepherds ("Today is born for you a savior," 2:11). "Salvation" is Jesus' mission. Mary rejoices to have this further confirmation of her son's destiny. But she has no inkling as to the price Jesus and she will pay for that salvation. What she also hears is that her son will be "a light of revelation to the Gentiles" (2:32), one of the titles Isaiah had given for the "Servant of the Lord" (Isaiah 42:6; 49:6). But how does Jesus become a source of light for the Gentiles? More questions for Mary to ponder. With Joseph she is "amazed at the things that were said" about the child (Luke 2:33).

A Cloud of Unknowing

After his spontaneous hymn about the child, Simeon has a word directed to Mary: "Behold [the word signals the solemnity of the revelation], this child is destined for the fall and rise of many in Israel, and for a sign that will be contradicted—and your own soul a sword shall pierce—that the thoughts of many hearts may be revealed" (Luke 2:34-35). Mary must have asked the Holy Spirit to help her understand these words:

Jesus will cause division among the people. Why? When Jesus was born, the angels sang about peace on earth. Is Simeon mistaken? How can both be true? And what does it mean that a sword will go through my soul? Lord, if this is true, give me the courage to stand firm for you and for Jesus. I know Jesus' suffering would be my suffering too, the kind of compassion that is doubly painful when there is nothing you can do to relieve the suffering of the one you love so much. And all of this, Simeon said, would open people's hearts to love or hate.

Mary's mind and heart must have been dizzy in a cloud of unknowing.

Then Anna the prophetess shows up, eighty-four years old, revered in the temple where she fasted and prayed night and day. I am reminded of a woman I once met, a professor at a large university, who had an exceptional gift of spending every night awake in the Newman Center church, praying, dusting, putting things in order, and taking only momentary catnaps when she got tired. Hers was truly a supernatural gift of the Holy Spirit. Apparently, prayer refreshed her better than sleep. (Her name, incidentally, was Mary.) But back to Anna. Nothing more is said of her than that she gave thanks to God and spoke of the child "to all who were awaiting the redemption of Israel" (Luke 2:38, NAB). With the aged Simeon, she represents Israel on the threshold of the New Testament, but she also prefigures the women prophets and evangelists in Acts who serve the gospel.

What did Mary think of Anna? I wonder if she didn't think

Anna was getting ahead of the story, because Jesus hadn't claimed or proved he was the Messiah yet. Anna was spilling the good news too soon. Perhaps that is why Luke tells us that the Holy Family retired to obscurity in Nazareth (Luke 2:39).

But before they did, if we merge with Matthew, we find them in Bethlehem, where the Evangelist has two important events to tell us, as we shall see in the next chapter.

....

Lord Jesus, you know how hard it is for me to let go and surrender to you all that is dear to me. In your mother's generous giving of you back to God, I see the kind of love I would like to have. Only you can work that kind of love in my heart through the power of the Holy Spirit. I hesitate even to ask it of you because I know that it is costly. But if you put your own love in my heart, I know it will bring me great joy. Amen.

FOR REFLECTION

1. How do I feel when someone I love suffers? How could Mary and the Holy Spirit help me turn my feelings into prayer?

2. A fifteen-year-old girl is suffering an advanced, disfiguring stage of cancer. Her vocation, like that of Jesus, is one of suffering. It takes faith and the Holy Spirit to see her life as a vocation. Do I see what I suffer as part of mine?

3. Life is a rhythm of holding and letting go. Mary's was too, for she held Jesus and then eventually had to let him go. How do I handle these two rhythms in my life?

Chapter 7

Receptivity

We change lenses now as we move to the Gospel of Matthew and read his take on the infancy of Jesus. Joseph has the lion's share here. After Joseph learned of the mystery of Mary's pregnancy and took her as his wife, Matthew shows us Jesus already born in Bethlehem and the Magi on pilgrimage from the East. The family resides in a house by now. One day, to their surprise, camels show up at their door. Traders from the other side of the Jordan, offering their wares? No, turbaned men who say they have come to honor the newborn king of the Jews. No poor shepherds these, offering palm-sized gifts of goat cheese. The Magi bring frankincense, myrrh, and gold.

How did they know of the birth? Unlike the shepherds who had learned from heavenly messengers, these strangers read the message in the heavens themselves, the stars. And they had passed through Jerusalem and asked King Herod where the newborn king was to be found. This detail must have sent a chill through Mary's heart. This is no longer Simeon hailing the Savior or Anna telling temple visitors about the child. The Magi's well-intentioned query means news has reached royal headquarters—and that might mean trouble. The Holy Spirit continues to hover over Mary's pondering. She begins to realize in a new way that Jesus is not meant for mere Christmas-card sweetness. He has already become a public and, in Herod's mind, a political figure.

How did the Holy Spirit teach Mary about handling fear? In the Scriptures, whenever a heavenly messenger appears with a revelation to someone, the messenger always begins with this reassurance: "Don't be afraid" (Genesis 15:1; Joshua 8:1; Judges 6:23; Luke 1:30). But this was no heavenly messenger. It was a threat from the cruel and unpredictable Herod. Could Mary still hear the words of Gabriel: "Don't be afraid, Mary" (Luke 1:30)? Is it possible for fear and trust to exist at the same time in a holy human heart? Were they both in Jesus' heart in Gethsemane? It seems so. I suspect that the Holy Spirit brought peace to Mary's heart when he enabled her to surrender once more. She was able to whisper to herself, "Whatever, let it be done," and in doing so, she was able to be totally present to her guests.

Significant in this story is Matthew's detail, "They saw the child with Mary his mother" (Matthew 2:11, NAB). Why doesn't Matthew mention Joseph too, since he has such a prominent role in these first two chapters? It can only be because the Evangelist wants to suggest the further fulfillment of the prophecy of Isaiah that the virgin would give birth to the Emmanuel king (1:23) while ignoring the father of this king, Ahaz (Isaiah 7:14). What did all this mean to Mary, bride of the Holy Spirit? If Jesus is King, she is the Queen Mother. She already knew this from the angel of the annunciation. But *how* is she to fulfill this role? For the time being, just in being a mother—and in this scene, that means welcoming the Magi and receiving their gifts with gratitude.

Hospitality was the law of the Middle East. Warmed and enlightened by the Holy Spirit, hospitality becomes a charism manifesting the presence of God (1 Corinthians 12:4-11). We can imagine Mary and Joseph scurrying to ready a meal and a place for the tired travelers to rest. But their greatest act of hospitality was not in their preparations. It was simply in their accepting the Magi's gifts.

Serving by Receiving

Receptivity: It looks like the opposite of service. But when one receives a gift, one receives the giver, and the greatest service one can do for the giver is to receive his gift. That is Luke's point in the Martha and Mary story (Luke 10:38-42). While Martha is busy preparing a meal for Jesus, Mary does Jesus the greater service by welcoming his word into her receiving heart.

Mary and Joseph here model the Holy Spirit's gift of receptivity for the rest of us. They receive the precious tokens of the strangers' devotion. And Mary receives the makers of a pilgrimage, the first of thousands to come.

It has taken me a long time to learn the gift of receiving. Of course, as a child I was told repeatedly to say, "Thank you," but to me at that age, the gift was more important than the love of the giver. I would run and play with the toy, oblivious of the giver. Later, as I grew older, when I gave gifts, I expected some kind of return—maybe not at once but eventually. I know lots of people who feel *obliged* to give a gift, as if they were paying the price for the relationship. It's Christmas, and Aunt Suzie will be expecting her gift and will be upset if she doesn't get it. If I receive a gift, am I expected to reciprocate? If so, this is barter, nothing more than an exchange of goods. If someone gives me a painting, will they be offended if I give it away, even after having kept it for a long time? And what about invitations? Am I offended if I am not invited? How easily gifts degenerate into payments.

I need to remind myself repeatedly that a true gift has no strings attached, whether I give it or receive it. The Magi expected nothing in return. In the story they disappeared just as freely as they came. Nor did Mary feel obligated by their gifts. If she gave them anything, it was not "in return." It was with full freedom and love and not to reduce the exchange to barter.

....

Holy Spirit, take my heart and teach it the grace of welcome and receptivity—to you, to Jesus, to the Father, in all the ways you come to me. But with Mary, also teach me how to be truly receptive to others, to receive not merely their gifts but their persons, to let them love me without feeling that I have to do anything more than see, accept, and welcome the love they show me in the gift. Amen.

FOR REFLECTION

1. The news that Herod had learned of the "newborn king" sent fear into Mary's heart. How do you think she handled this fear? How do you handle your fears?

2. When confronted with unexpected and troubling news, are you able to bracket your feelings for the moment in order to be present to the persons you are attending to? How would reflecting on Mary's situation help?

3. How do you handle gift giving and receiving? Do you get caught up in the barter mentality, obliging you to reciprocate when you receive a gift or to expect gifts in return for your gifts? Pray that you may have the grace, like Mary, to give freely and receive freely.

Chapter 8

Flight

Joseph's touch was more than gentle when he shook Mary awake. "Quick," he said. "Pack up and grab Jesus. We're getting out of here at once."

"Why?" the startled Mary asked him. "And what's the hurry?"

"I'll explain later. We're in danger."

An exchange something like this one must have occurred after an angel told Joseph in a dream that "Herod is going to search for the child to destroy him" (Matthew 2:13, NAB). And where was he told to go? "To Egypt."

"Egypt? The country that enslaved our ancestors, that killed our firstborn sons?"

"Yes, Joseph, it's safer there than in the shadow of Herod's sword."

So they slipped through Bethlehem's slumbering streets toward the desert road, watched only by the stars.

No word is recorded of Joseph or Mary before or during the flight. But again the Holy Spirit helps Mary to ponder. And there are more questions:

If Jesus is God's son, if he is the Messiah, what a strange way for him to begin his career. He is the Anointed One? Does it have to be so contradictory to his status? But then, look what happened to baby Moses when that other Herod, Pharaoh of

Egypt, was killing off the baby boys of our people. The Lord saved him in a basket, and the boy grew up to lead our people to freedom. Is it going to be the same with Jesus? But how can he save Israel now if he grows up and lives in Egypt? Will he get crowned king there and lead an invasion?

The Holy Spirit does not give Mary answers. He guides her questions and strengthens her trust as she rides a donkey in the night through an arid, unknown land toward an even lesser-known country and a destiny that seems to be anything but what the angel had promised her. Mary is literally journeying through the "dark night" of which the mystics would later speak. She is walking by faith and not by sight (2 Corinthians 5:7).

As we travel with Mary in this scene, we are invited to let the Holy Spirit hover over our unanswered questions. The Spirit can show us that far from diverting us from our journey, such questions are really signposts of the authentic route, since they prod us to trust—and "trust" is the name of the road. The Lord doesn't give us a road map of the journey ahead. He says only, "Follow me." Mary is learning this as each page of her life is turned.

The trio is a refugee family. Mary had no idea that God was fashioning this refugee family to be itself a refuge for generations to come. In Nepal we welcomed a family of Christian refugees from Sri Lanka. In an irony that appeared to me to be divine, the family's name was "Joseph." We saw the relief in their eyes that they had found temporary shelter, making me think of these words from Psalm 36: "To man and beast you give protection. / O LORD, how precious is your love" (verses 7-8). But I could also read in the father's eyes the anxiety that must have been in the eyes of Joseph and Mary as they sought entry into Egypt.

Refugees like Their Ancestors

Imaginative authors later penned stories about the Holy Family's journey—trees bending in adoration as the family passed by or the boy Jesus turning a clay bird into a live one—but these are illusions born of an unreal Christology. Real life was not like that. Joseph found himself job hunting, and Mary tried to bargain at the market in a language she did not know. How easy it was for storekeepers to take advantage of this couple, so naïve about Egyptian ways. Seeking freedom from Herod, they found themselves like their ancestors who had been slaves, trapped in their own inadequacy and Egyptian wiles. Again Mary pondered: "What was it like for my ancestors to live as slaves in this land? To ply mud and straw to quotas impossible to reach? At least it's not that bad for us. We're only trying to keep our heads above the immigration floodwaters."

Not long after they settled in Nile country, word arrived of Herod's slaughter of the children in Bethlehem. Mary must have rebelled in anger and then melted into weeping and sobbing. She was like Rachel, who mourned her children as they were dragged into exile (Jeremiah 31:15), except that the children in Bethlehem were literally no more. Grief is not sin. It is the normal response of the human heart that God has made (Jesus wept at the tomb of Lazarus, John 11:35). But at some point, Mary must have thought, "These children died because of Jesus." Then she would have felt the sword Simeon had foretold plunging deeper into her heart. Of course, the day would come when Jesus would die for these same children, but that was still hidden from Mary's eyes.

If it was because of Jesus that the innocents died, did the tragedy strike Mary with a flash of guilt? This kind of guilt can haunt the soldier who survives a battle when the buddy at his side dies— "Why him and not me?" It would haunt my Uncle Gene for years after he hit a child who dashed in front of his car and died instantly. When regret at innocent tragedy becomes guilt—false guilt—it can cripple and even lead to death, as St. Paul says (2 Corinthians 7:10). How did the Holy Spirit guide Mary to deal with this moment? Her tears became intercession for the child victims, their mothers and fathers, and yes, even for Herod and his henchmen. The Holy Spirit knows how to transform something negative into something positive. He will do so for us if we let him hover over our chaos, as Mary surely did.

....

Anxiety, fear, frustration, discomfort, homesickness, grief, false guilt: Lord, when I experience these, remind me that I am not alone. Your Holy Spirit is with me, and with his comfort and strength, I can praise you at all times, as Mary did, and turn what is negative into something positive for your glory. Amen.

FOR REFLECTION

1. Were there times in your life when you journeyed through a "dark night" with more questions than answers? What was it like? Did the experience help you to find God?

2. Have you ever experienced being in a "foreign land" literally or figuratively, when you felt lost, homesick, or insecure? In what ways did it help you grow in faith and trust in God?

3. Have you ever been tormented by false guilt? How could Mary help you in such a situation?

Chapter 9

Journey

Joseph was a dreamer. Four times St. Matthew tells us that God gave him directions in his dreams: to take Mary as his wife because she was pregnant by the Holy Spirit (1:20), to take the family and flee to Egypt (2:13), to return to Israel (2:19-20), and then to go not to Bethlehem but to Nazareth (2:22).

Herod is dead. So the Lord tells Joseph to lead his family out of Egypt. Were Joseph and Mary aware that they were reliving the history of their people? Doubtless it was part of Mary's pondering. Sold as a slave, the Old Testament Joseph was forced to go to Egypt. Exiled, too, in Egypt, the New Testament Joseph will lead his family out. The old Joseph was an interpreter of dreams. The new Joseph received God's word in dreams. Moses had fled to the desert from Pharaoh who wanted to kill him. When Pharaoh died, the Lord told Moses to return, "for those who sought your life are dead" (Exodus 4:19). Matthew applies the phrase to Herod, whose demise opens the path for Jesus' return (2:20). Maybe Matthew was not the first to think of this replay of sacred history. Whether Mary was the first, we don't know, but certainly a woman whose only book was the Scriptures would have thought of passages like that of Hosea relating the Lord's description of the Exodus: "Out of Egypt I called my son" (11:1, NAB). Israel was collectively the Lord's adoptive son; Jesus was God's Son in person.

Living Water in the Desert

It must have been a relief and a joy to Mary to learn that she, Joseph, and the child Jesus were going home. Sometimes natives of a particular place refer to their home as "God's country." (Drivers coming into Hondo, Texas, are welcomed with this sign: "This is God's country. Don't drive through it like hell.") But in a true sense, Israel was, and is, God's country, the promised land of the Bible. It would be a long journey for the family, longer than the one from Bethlehem to Egypt, because Joseph had been told to go farther north to Galilee. Herod had died, but his son, Archelaus, was ruling Judea and Samaria. He was the kind of king who would send his cavalry to kill three thousand Jews in the temple during Passover, and he would eventually be deposed by the emperor. Joseph was well advised to go to Galilee.

What were Mary's thoughts during this journey of several weeks? As the family trekked through the Sinai, she had plenty of time to think about the journey of her ancestors, much longer than hers, through this barren land. The Holy Spirit, who would one day lead Jesus into the desert for forty days (Mark 1:12-13), was giving the boy Jesus, his mother, and Joseph a foretaste of desert living. But however harsh the terrain, however racked with thirst their throats, the Holy Spirit was showing Mary that even in the desert, there was living water. It was the water that welled up in the heart of the pilgrim (John 4:14) and made the journey bearable. Crossing through Archelaus' restive Judea and Samaria, the family was flanked by uncertainty on every side. It must have been a great relief, physically and emotionally, to finally arrive in the village of Nazareth, where Mary had relatives and there was at least the protection of obscurity and distance from the turmoil in Judea.

In our lives, too, there are times when we find ourselves in the desert. Our first thought may be that God has abandoned us, since we are no longer walking in the garden of his delights. Of course, if sin has entered our lives, then we have reason to believe that this is so. But if not, then we need to realize that God has called us, as he called the Holy Family, into the desert as a necessary leg of our journey. Yes, a call. "I will lead her into the desert and speak to her heart" (Hosea 2:16, NAB). Left in the desert, we will search desperately for the living water, the Holy Spirit, who refreshes in a way no earthly water can. Mary will show us where the living water is. As she knew the way to the village well to which she went to draw water morning and evening, so she knows where the living water of the Holy Spirit flows abundantly. And when we find it, the desert does not change, but we open our eyes to its beauty and embrace it with love.

It should be clear from all of this that the life of the Spirit, the life that Mary led—or rather the life of Mary that the Spirit led—is a journey. Mary's was a journey to Ein Karem, to Bethlehem, to Egypt, to Nazareth. But it was also an inward journey led by the Holy Spirit. "Those who are led by the Spirit of God are children of God" (Romans 8:14, NAB). "Walk in the Spirit and you will certainly not gratify the desires of the flesh" (Galatians 5:16). "If we live in the Spirit, let us also follow the Spirit" (Galatians 5:25, NAB). These are all journey images.

Our life, too, is a journey. We pass through hilltops and valleys, gardens and deserts. Do not let the terrain beguile or depress you. Instead, let each changing scene be a page of the book that the Holy Spirit is using to teach you. Mary was the first one to be taught by the Spirit in this way. If you ask her, with her experience she will show you what God is saying to you on each page.

....

Dear Lord, I see now that my coming home to you will mean at times crossing a desert. Let me not be disheartened by the heat, the blowing sand, the thirst. Remind me that there is living water in the desert I must traverse, and may Mary show me the way to the well. Amen.

FOR REFLECTION

1. Think of a time when you experienced extreme thirst. How can this be an image of your soul thirsting for the living water, the Holy Spirit?

2. Mary knows where the living water is. How can you allow her to show you the way to it?

3. Do you ever get homesick for heaven? Pray for the grace to long for that final reunion when you will see the Lord (and his mother) face-to-face.

Chapter 10

Ordinary Time

About those next years in Nazareth, the gospels guard a reverent silence. It might thus seem presumptuous to intrude. Yet part of the mystery of the incarnation is those years in which Mary, mother in the Holy Spirit, watched and helped her son grow. I can only muse on my own early years to get some idea of what it was like in the home at Nazareth.

My earliest memory is that of my great-grandfather, who died when I was two-and-a-half years old. I remember his periodic visits to the kitchen, where life was baked and broken. I also remember his sunken face as he lay in the coffin—my first experience of life's end as I was experiencing its beginning. As she held me on her hip at the coffin, my Aunt Margaret explained to me what had happened to Great-grandpa. When one of Jesus' relatives died—perhaps one who had held him, played with him, and given him hugs and kisses—the child Jesus encountered the mystery of death. So Mary must have explained to Jesus what had happened to the relative whose death was the first that Jesus witnessed. What did she say? Belonging to the most devout of the day, she surely believed in the resurrection, so she must have told Jesus about the promise of life to come. Little did she know at that time how Jesus would conquer death by rising from the dead himself, her firstborn who was the "firstborn" of all who would rise (Colossians 1:18). But enlightened by the Holy Spirit,

Mary knew God had a plan for her son and that she had a role in it, although it unfolded only day by day.

There were many things my mother did for me. My greatest frustration in those early years was not being able to tie my shoes. Mama did that for me until I finally learned. When I stepped on a nail, driving it into the sole of my foot, she was there to treat me. She would take me to the kitchen window to admire the burnt-orange sunsets that crowned the western hills. Mary surely did things like that for Jesus. When one day he would say, "Look at the lilies, how they grow!" he was echoing his love for nature's beauty that he had learned from his mother. Most mothers do these things naturally. But what was it like for Mary to be guided by the divine artist, the Holy Spirit?

My mother was not Hispanic, but the Spanish language was her hobby. As I bobbed around her in the kitchen, she would teach me the Spanish words for "broom," "table," "knife," "fork," and other things in sight. Then she would test me by saying the word, and I would run to or point out the object. Mary probably taught Jesus his Aramaic vocabulary in similar ways. What a joy it must have been for her when Jesus showed her the wooden toy he had made in Joseph's workshop.

One of my mother's muffled anxieties was caused by the fact that we had guns in the house for hunting. That was an unquestioned custom in ranch homes of those days. We were well trained from childhood in gun safety, but as I look back on those years, I wonder how much my mother worried about us when we left the house with a rifle in our hands. She knew all too well of hunting accidents, some of which had been fatal. The Holy Family's household was not so provisioned, of course, but when Jesus went out to play with the village children, did Mary at times worry that he might fall out of a tree he had climbed and break an arm or leg? The fact that he was the Son of God didn't free him from having to learn how to do things, and that sometimes meant learning from his mistakes. For example, did he always tie a knot right the first time? His divine nature did not make him a human marionette. Jesus "grew in wisdom" (Luke 2:52), and that meant going from less wisdom to more. Mary watched that growth and prayed that he would have more wisdom rather than less as he perched on the top limb of that tree. I fancy the Holy Spirit inspired her prayer for him rather than numbing her anxiety.

But most significant of all, Mary taught Jesus to pray. He who in eternity lived in constant union with the Father had to learn how to pray as a human being. She taught him verses from the psalms— praising God for the rising sun, for the blessing of the land, for help in distress, for peace, and yes, before going to sleep, that verse of Psalm 31: "Into your hands I commend my spirit" (verse 6, NAB), which Jesus one day would say to the Father as he handed his spirit over in death. And if the Holy Spirit was with Mary as she prayed, then she had already experienced what Paul would later describe in these words: "The Spirit comes to the aid of our weakness; for we do not know how to pray as we ought, but the Spirit himself intercedes with inexpressible groanings. And the one who searches hearts knows what is the intention of the Spirit, because he intercedes for the holy ones according to God's will" (Romans 8:26-27). There were times, then, when Mary's prayer surpassed her understanding because the Holy Spirit was praying to the Father in her.

The Holy Spirit not only guided Mary's mothering of Jesus; he also shaped her spousal love for Joseph. Theirs was a marital union but of a unique kind. In a Christian tradition that reigned until the Reformation, Joseph not only had no role in the conception of Jesus, but he respected the once-for-all consecration of her body by abstaining from sexual intimacy with her for the rest of his life. The Holy Spirit who conceived Jesus in Mary must have graced Joseph with an understanding and joyful acceptance of his celibate role in the face of Mary's espousal to the Holy Spirit. Mary, too, embraced her unique vocation and sought no other pleasure than following the lead of the Spirit as he danced daily with her. Some may scoff at this celibate union as a denigration of marriage. No one, of course, draws the conclusion from the Holy Family that the ideal marriage should be virginal. But it does point to the fact that marriage is more than sex; it is sacrificial love, commitment, and self-giving service that make a marriage work.

Total Gift of Self

Surely there was a great mutual love between Mary and Joseph. But as Antoine de Saint-Exupéry wrote in *The Little Prince*, love is not looking at one another but looking together in the same direction. For the holy couple, that direction was Jesus. Blessed John Paul II often said that the human person finds fulfillment in the total gift of self. Surely nowhere was this found in greater measure than in the Holy Family, reflection of the self-gift of the Father, Son, and Holy Spirit in the life of the Trinity.

The sanctification of ordinariness—such is the lesson of the hidden life. For Mary this meant rising early each morning, fetching water, cooking, cleaning, washing clothes, sewing, chatting with a neighbor, visiting the sick, shopping at the market, or occasionally chopping wood when Joseph and Jesus were overloaded with carpentry work. This, too, was part of her domestic Pentecost. "If your gift is service, let it be with the strength that God provides" (1 Peter 4:10). Later statuary would show her with her hands joined in prayer. However accurate such a depiction of her role as intercessor, I fancy her arms as muscular and her hands as rugged.

The Church celebrates ordinary and extraordinary times. The extraordinary are the major seasons: Advent, Christmas, Lent, and Easter. But the longest season, the one in which green vestments are worn by the priest, is simply called "Ordinary Time." Most of Mary's life was ordinary time. Certainly there were the major feasts: Passover, the Feast of Weeks (Pentecost), and the Feast of Tabernacles. These were joyous celebrations of the major events in the history of her people. But they were simply mountaintop moments of relief from the valleys and even the deserts of daily life. They were routine-breakers, lifting the people to closer union with God. But what about ordinary time, the time in which we live most often? Mary shows us how even daily routine and inglorious chores can be "sacraments" of union with God if we let the Holy Spirit bathe them in God's love—or as St. Thérèse of Lisieux would say, if we do ordinary things with extraordinary love.

....

Mary, teach me to pray as you taught your child, Jesus, and show me God's glory in ordinary things. Remind me that nothing need escape the embrace of the Father's love, no matter how trivial or dreary. As the Holy Spirit transformed your simple, everyday duties, making them bright threads in the tapestry he was weaving of your life, pray that he do the same for me. I want to do ordinary things with extraordinary love. Amen.

FOR REFLECTION

1. If Mary is the mother of each of us, she must delight in watching us grow in the Spirit, just as she watched Jesus grow. But spiritual maturity is also becoming a little child in trustful abandon. How can Mary lead you in such a way?

2. What anxieties do you have for your loved ones? Ask Mary to share her wisdom on how to deal with those feelings.

3. Think of the ordinary things you do regularly. Ask Mary to show you how to do them with extraordinary love.

Chapter 11

Questions

The home in Nazareth was not a contemplative monastery. There was plenty of prayer there, of course, but Jewish tradition also called for pilgrimages for the major feasts, Passover being the principal one. So Mary, Joseph, and the growing Jesus, seasoned travelers even to a foreign land, made a yearly pilgrimage up to Jerusalem for the feast of Passover.

During the three-day journey with scores of other pilgrims, the Holy Family would have joined in singing the "going up" psalms, like the one that begins like this: "I rejoiced when they said to me, / 'Let us go up to the house of the LORD'" (Psalm 122:1). The joy of the pilgrims at times was so great that one of the psalms says it turned the mastic-tree valley into a place of springs (Psalm 84:7). Pilgrims choked the streets of the holy city for a whole week, until finally they broke up into caravans and took the road home. Men and women would travel separately during the day, and families would be reunited as night fell. Jesus was at Bar-Mitzvah age, which means that he could have been either with his mother or his father, and this is the traditional explanation of why both Joseph and Mary thought he was with the other.

Imagine the couple coming together at dusk only to find that Jesus was not with either of them, and then scurrying around among relatives and friends and still not finding him. Panic at the loss of a child—a panic that has been felt by many parents in our time under oppressive regimes when a son or daughter disappears and never returns. There is a Marian litany that invokes Mary as "Mother of the disappeared." Even parents whose children do not return on time at night experience anxiety. Mary certainly did. She was a mother, a Jewish mother, and the mother-child bond is the strongest of human ties, surpassing even that of spouses. It is important to realize that having been overshadowed by the Holy Spirit was no guarantee that Mary would be free of emotional suffering during her life. That is an important lesson for us. The Holy Spirit comes to us not to disable our cares but to enable us to cope.

Hence we are permitted to imagine the kaleidoscope of thoughts that ran through her mind and feelings that ran through her heart during the day-long trip back to Jerusalem: "What went wrong? I last saw him with Joseph. Why did I presume Jesus was with him? Should I have checked again? Where is he now? Has something horrible happened to him? I know he is an adventurous boy and willing to take risks. Maybe he ventured too far!"

Relief, Then Anger

And there he was in the temple, safe and sound ("Thank God!"). But instead of seeing him playing with other kids in the large court of the women, they saw him immersed in a circle of elders—teachers of the law—listening to them and firing questions at them. This astonished Mary and Joseph. What was Mary's response? Relief, then anger. Mary, angry? Why not? Jesus had taken off on his own without saying a word, and any human parent would rapidly go through two emotions: relief that the child is safe, then anger at his presumed foolishness and lack of concern for his parents. In a nature film shot in Africa, a mother elephant rescues her calf from his adolescent stupidity of getting stuck in a mud hole. Once she has gotten him out safely and has examined him carefully with her trunk, she uses it to give him a resounding slap. Mary's twofold emotion of relief and anger blurted out in her question: "Son, why have you done this to us? Your father and I have been looking for you with great anxiety" (Luke 2:48, NAB).

Jesus' answer was both typically that of a teenager and that of the Son of God: "Why were you looking for me? Did you not know I must be in my Father's house?" (Luke 2:49, NAB). It was not so much the assertion of teenage independence that shocked them; it was the opaque reason he gave for it. Perhaps this is what Mary was thinking:

> His father's house? That was the point of my question. Your father's house is in Nazareth, and we should have been there by now! But no, he meant something else by it. He called the temple "my Father's house." He did not say, "our Father's house," which would still not be an adequate reason for leaving the family, but any Jew within earshot would not have questioned the theology of what he said. But he said, "*my* Father's house," as if he owned the place, or at least as if his father did.

In Luke's gospel the angel had called her child "Son of the Most High" (1:32), so this was not new for Mary. But like the faint, distant groan of an oncoming train, she heard in the boy's answer what she knew would eventually be coming: separation. Though he would spend another eighteen years with her, Jesus' answer was an early warning that he was given to her that she might give him to others. He was not only son of Mary. He was Messiah and Son of God.

Luke gives us the understanding that Jesus' detour to the temple was a single, exceptional event, for he concludes Jesus' childhood stories with the note that he went down with Mary and Joseph to Nazareth "and was obedient to them" (2:51, NAB). It appears, then, that Jesus freely and lovingly hid any manifestation of his divinity or claim to it under the ordinariness of the village life of a carpenter's family. To say that is to say that he and his mother were perfectly human, the only members of the human race to whom the word *perfectly* could apply. It took a God to show us how to be human, and a woman empowered by the Holy Spirit to show us that it can happen to someone who is not God. And in their company, empowered by the Holy Spirit, it can happen to you and me.

....

Jesus, you have given me your mother to help me deal with the worries and anxieties I have about my loved ones. Some of my loved ones are sick, some do not know you and your Church, some have wandered from your fold, some are caught in addictions. Mary, you who went through the agony of losing your child, help me when I am overwhelmed with anxieties, and teach me how to turn them into prayer. Amen.

FOR REFLECTION

1. Have you ever experienced the anxiety of missing a loved one? How about a son or daughter past their curfew? How did you handle it? Did you think of joining in Mary's prayer as she searched for her son?

2. How do you understand this sentence: "The Holy Spirit comes to us not to disable our cares but to enable us to cope"?

3. In Jesus' separation and in his answer, his mother experienced the "otherness" of her son, not just his human otherness (which happens with every mother as her child grows into adulthood), but his divine otherness—"He is not only my son, he is God's Son." What do you think this meant for Mary? How do you think she coped with this truth?

Chapter 12

Letting Go

We were halfway through a crisp January night in 1942 when the train we were waiting for pulled into the Southern Pacific station. Given the wartime urgency, it was to be more of a hesitation than a stop, but it allowed my mother and the rest of us brief words and hugs with my brother Charlie before the train began rolling him on to Marine boot camp in San Diego. Charlie and his buddy, Gene, already uniformed, leaned out of one of the car doors to wave a final good-bye. Indeed, it was final. It was the last time any of us saw him, as he fell on the beach of Tarawa, with Gene, less than two years later. I was too young to appreciate what my mother was going through at that midnight parting, but I have some idea now. The mother-son bond is the deepest of human attachments, and the pain must have been wrenching.

I saw her reaction too when my other brother, Frank, and his new bride drove away in a 1940 Chevy to go to pilot-training school. And I saw her tears when I climbed aboard a Missouri-Pacific train three years later to enter the Marianists. My mother was being trained in the most difficult of human choices: letting go. Every mother has to learn the meaning of *fiat*, certainly more than once.

What about the day when Jesus told his mother that he was leaving to be baptized by John the Baptist in the Judean Jordan?

The greater the love, the greater the pain of separation. But listening to Jesus over the years of the hidden life and watching him, she had come to understand that his mission was not exactly what everybody was thinking the Messiah would be and do. His kingdom was to be a spiritual one, beginning in people's hearts.

And what about the Romans? Well, Roman soldiers had the right to commandeer any Jew to carry their packs one mile. I can imagine that one day, Mary saw a Roman soldier grab Jesus and make him his "one-mile mule." Jesus carried the soldier's pack and talked with him about God and about loving people. At the end of the mile, the soldier reached for his pack, as the law obliged him to, but Jesus said, "No. Let me carry it for you another mile." Stunned, the soldier asked, "Why would you do such a thing?" "Because I love you, and God does too," Jesus said. "I enjoy carrying other people's burdens." And Jesus went on to tell the soldier about his plans for the kingdom of God, about forgiveness of sins and forgiveness of others, about peace out of justice and love, and all of this because God is a loving and forgiving Father. Suddenly the relation of Jew and Gentile was on a totally different plane. And Mary nodded when Jesus told her about the encounter. She understood, if not fully.

So Jesus' plans for the kingdom cushioned the parting for Mary, as her heart was one with his about the more important and urgent mission that he had been given. But cushioning the separation did not mean removing its pain. How does a mother react when a son leaves her on a mission she knows he must fulfill? For twelve years I had been assigned to the Marianists' works in San Antonio, so I was able to visit my aging mother frequently. Then on Good Friday of 1972, my provincial called me, asking me to move to St. Louis to head our seminary there. I knew this would be hard on my mother, because now I would be at a great distance, with few chances to visit her. Neither she nor I knew that she had less than two years to live. As soon as I had a chance, I drove to the ranch. "Mama," I said, "I've got something important to tell you." She left the pot she was tending on the stove, wiped her hands, and said, "Well, let's sit down." We did, on the couch together. I broke the news as gently as I could. She took a few silent moments to absorb it, then turned to me with a big tear rolling down her left cheek but a smile on her face and said, "Well, when you put your hand to the plow, it won't do to look back" (Luke 9:62). I feel certain that such was Jesus' parting from Mary. It was the mysterious wedding of pain and joy in loving sacrifice. Tears. A smile. And the word of God. Tears for the pain, smile for the support, and the word for the anchor.

All of us have to learn the art of letting go, but it is especially challenging for mothers. How many mothers have tried to "manage" their children's married lives! Instead of letting go, they want to continue the control they had when their children were young.

In the spiritual life, this natural compulsion of a parent to live their children's lives may carry over in a way that may look holy—but may not be. I mean the parent who is overwrought because her child is wandering into evil ways. She prays fervently and constantly for the wandering to stop, but there is a hidden demand that the child convert exactly as she wants it *right now*. Please understand me. This type of anxious love has made saints of countless mothers—St. Monica, the mother of Augustine, being the best known. But there comes a point—and I have helped many a mother to see it—where God wants her to release her offspring into his hands and leave them there. This does not mean ceasing to pray; it does means letting go at a deeper level than ever by surrendering the loved one completely to the Lord. This kind of prayer brings the anguished parent herself into a closer union with God as it brings her intercession into a deeper level. A brother priest told me that he suffered that anxiety for his family as he prayed, but then one day as others prayed over him, he heard the Lord say, "Don't you think I care even more about your family than you do?"

That is what Mary realized as she let go of Jesus: "The Father cares more about him than I ever possibly could. *Fiat.*"

Jesus' New Family

So after thirty years with his mother, Jesus left Nazareth and began his public ministry. The synoptic gospels record only one incident involving Mary during those three years. Jesus' relatives took Mary along with them to check out what Jesus was up to. Mark 3:31-35 indicates that those relatives thought that Jesus was too radical (like the CEO father who wants to retrieve his son from protesting wage discrimination). Or perhaps they thought he was out of his mind and that the family's reputation might be tarnished. Another possible translation of this passage from the Greek is that Jesus' relatives were concerned that the crowd was out of control and might endanger him. But in Matthew, Jesus' relatives just want to speak with Jesus. Again, we are left to color in the spaces as we wish. I fancy cousin James wanting to repro-gram Jesus in order to take him home and put him back in his carpenter shop. So he sends him this message: "Your mother and your brothers are standing outside, asking to speak with you." In a culture in which family loyalties had eminent domain, Jesus' response must have shocked everyone: "'Who is my mother? Who are my brothers?' And pointing to his disciples, he said, 'Here are my mother and my brothers. For whoever does the will of my heavenly Father is my brother and sister and mother'" (Matthew 12:48-50; see also Luke 8:19-21).

What was Mary's role in this scene? Was she dragged along? Was she concerned for Jesus' safety? (After all, the crowds in Nazareth had tried to throw him off the cliff; see Luke 4:29-30.) And how did Jesus' response affect her? Jesus was saying that his disciples were his family now. That means that the spiritual bond Jesus forms with those who believe in him trumps blood relationships. If Jesus had spent thirty years with Mary and shared his dream with her, Mary could hardly have been ignorant of that reality. From the evidence of the New Testament, it seems that the "brothers" of Jesus for a long time did not believe in him (John 7:5), but they finally did (Acts 1:14). But Mary was the first believer, and Jesus would one day say that whoever hears the word of God and acts on it is more blessed than the mother who suckled him (Luke 11:27-28). Far from being a put-down of Mary, the blessing really applied in the first place to Mary, more blessed because she believed than that she bore Jesus.

If we read this family-intrusion scene in the light of Mary's fullness of the Holy Spirit, I imagine that when these "brothers" told Mary that they wanted to find Jesus, she replied, "Jesus is right in what he is doing. But I will go along with you, and you will see." In the film *Jesus of Nazareth* (the uncut version at least), director Franco Zeffirelli, in a stroke of genius, has young John, the Beloved Disciple, slip away from the twelve and find Jesus' mother. He drops to his knees, looks with awe into her eyes, and says: "*You are his mother!*" To which she replies, "Whoever follows Jesus can become his mother and brother and sister." That scene brilliantly captures Mary's understanding of Jesus' mission—and the shock Jesus' words might cause us otherwise—by having the Lord's words on the lips of Mary herself.

Luke tells us that there was a group of women disciples who also followed Jesus and his men disciples, taking care of their needs (8:2-3). Was Mary among them? The gospels don't tell us. Her first duty was to be with Joseph, particularly if age and infirmity were overtaking him. However, when he died, she would have been free to join the other women following Jesus. Is it possible that Jesus stayed those long years at home because Joseph died early and Jesus continued his carpentry to support his mother? These are just some of the questions that go unanswered as we read the gospels.

And another question: Why after the infancy gospels does Mary virtually disappear from the synoptic gospels? Precisely, I believe, because the Evangelists want to follow Jesus' lead in stressing that the bond of faith trumps the bonds of blood. She will appear again in John at the beginning (2:1-12) and at the end of his public ministry (19:25-27), but for the time being, she is in the wings, not on stage. Nevertheless, we will see her as a central figure at the beginning of Acts where, after the ascension of Jesus, she will be the closest reminder of him and where, having experienced her Pentecost at the conception of Jesus, she will show them how to respond to the gift of the Holy Spirit.

....

Lord Jesus, baptize me again with your Holy Spirit so that I may enter into your passion for the mission the Father gave you. May it consume my life as it consumed your mother's. And when the sacrifices it involves confront me, if there are tears, then let me also smile with the joy of sacrifice and find strength and comfort in your word. Amen.

FOR REFLECTION

1. In your life so far, what has been the most difficult experience of letting go? As you reflect on it now, how would turning to Mary have helped you?

2. Mary in her humility was good at deflecting her glory back to God or to others. If you are kin to a celebrity or a very important person, do you boast of that instead of praying for that person? How can you grow in humility like Mary?

3. How do you see your relation to your natural family and your spiritual family, the Church? How can you grow in love for your brothers and sisters in Christ?

Chapter 13

Intercessor

As we turn to the Gospel of John, we need to switch lenses again. Better still, we need a telescope. The stars are beautiful to the naked eye, but what wonders greet us when we can see them up close! There is a challenge of mystery in every passage of the Fourth Gospel, and scholars for centuries have explored its depths. So in this meditation, we will select what we consider to be the best way to understand the wedding feast of Cana (John 2:1-11) from the viewpoint of Mary and the Holy Spirit.

"On the third day there was a wedding in Cana in Galilee, and the mother of Jesus was there" (John 2:1, NAB). Scholars ask, "What is it the third day from?" Opinions differ, but I strongly suspect John is suggesting that this scene is symbolic of what is going to be achieved on the third day of Jesus' passion—the resurrection, Jesus' wedding with his bride, the Church. At Cana Mary and Jesus are the main characters. What was Mary's role? The text simply says she was *there*. Unlike the case with Jesus and his disciples, the text does not say that she was among the invited guests. We can guess that she may have been in on the planning of the wedding and in charge of the waiters, as is suggested by the fact that she is able to direct them to Jesus. So she seems to have had some responsibility for the celebration, and if this is the case, then she would have shared in the embarrassment created by the last drop of wine. In any case, she is alert to the crisis and knows where to turn.

"They have no wine," she whispers to Jesus (John 2:3, NAB). This is no mere statement of fact; it is a mother's request, as is clear from Jesus' response. But there is a deeper level of meaning in Mary's words. The prophets had foretold that the messianic age would be characterized by an abundance of wine (Isaiah 55:1; Jeremiah 31:12; Joel 2:19, 24; 3:18). In the synoptic gospels, Jesus says that his mission is to bring new wine (Matthew 9:17), and Luke cleverly says that the gift of the Holy Spirit at Pentecost makes some of the bystanders think that the disciples were drunk on new wine (Acts 2:13). So when Mary says they have no wine, at the symbolic level she is saying that her people lack that new wine. The messianic banquet will be a disaster if they don't have the Holy Spirit.

Jesus then addresses his mother as "woman," which is not the way a son would address his mother, even in Hebrew or Aramaic. On the surface it looks like a rebuke of Mary, especially since the rest of his response looks like a refusal of her request. But John the Evangelist is giving us a flashback to the Garden of Eden, when God put enmity between the "woman" and Satan, and promised that through her offspring, Satan's power would be crushed (Genesis 3:15). How did Mary respond to the title "woman" and to Jesus' initial refusal? We don't know whether she realized that Jesus was, in fact, calling her the New Eve, thus fulfilling that prophecy. But either Mary did not take Jesus' response as a refusal, or she wanted to press her request by having the waiters come directly to Jesus to ask him what they should do. We do know the rest of the story. Jesus turns the water into wine in an abundance that would be enough for several wedding feasts. The headwaiter thinks it is the bridegroom who surprisingly has provided the better wine and, at the level of John's irony, he credits the wrong bridegroom. Jesus is the bridegroom, and his miracle launches his own wedding feast with the Church.

The New Wine of the Spirit

"You have kept the better wine until now" (John 2:10). For the headwaiter, this wine is the best yet. At the deeper level, Jesus is the one who brings the Holy Spirit to a thirsting people, and he does so at Mary's bidding.

Mary, then, appears here as intercessor, and she is successful in meeting the needs of the guests at the feast. In fact, there is much more wine than necessary. I sometimes think of God as a sloppy host, who keeps pouring after we have said "when," as if to say, "Why didn't you bring a bigger glass?"

Wine invites fluency, song, and dance. In my seminary days in Europe, it was evident that on the days when we had wine, the volume of chatter and laughter at our table doubled. In Spain, during a month in which I sought to perfect my Spanish, I was invited by my Marianist hosts at a festive dinner to stand and give a speech—in Spanish, of course. I demurred for as long as I could, but the wine they had plied me with freed me of my shyness, and I gave the most fluent speech in Spanish that I had ever given until then (at least I thought so!). God gives wine to gladden our hearts (Psalm 104:15), but the Beloved's love is better than wine (Song of Songs 1:2, 4; 4:10). When that love is poured into our hearts by the Holy Spirit (Romans 5:5), we taste what the Fathers of the Church called the "sober intoxication of God."

Scripture never says that God is intoxicated, but there are times when it describes his joy in terms that fit the feast of the wine harvest: "He will rejoice over you with gladness, / and renew you in his love, / He will sing joyfully because of you, / as one sings at festivals" (Zephaniah 3:17-18, NAB). If God is so happy to be in love with his people that he sings as one sings at festivals, how does one sing at festivals? Well, I know one way. At a "yodelerfest" in Fribourg, Switzerland, some four thousand yodelers descended on the town, first in a parade of yodeling teams, then in a yodeling competition that night. With my fellow seminarians, I sat in on the event until finally we left them to their singing and yodeling, which lasted into the wee hours of the morning. Our seminary was built on a cliff overlooking the Sarine River; together with the opposite cliff, a canyon-megaphone formed for sounds from the *basse-ville* or lower city. I was awakened at five o'clock in the morning by a yodeler yodeling from far off in the *basse-ville!* That's the way one sings at festivals.

There must have been plenty of singing and dancing at Cana once the guests had tasted the new and better wine. Just as Mary was there when that sign of the Spirit was poured out, so she would be present at Pentecost when the Spirit himself would descend and intoxicate the praying community.

....

Lord Jesus, although I am two millennia distant from the marriage feast of Cana, whenever I taste of the Holy Spirit, I know that I am drinking the better wine that you provide. Through the intercession of the woman who first received that Spirit when you came to earth, grant me a new outpouring at this very moment. Let me experience the sober intoxication of the Holy Spirit so that I may know you more deeply and be empowered, like Mary, to sing your praises and serve you more faithfully. Amen.

FOR REFLECTION

1. When you run out of human resources, how likely are you to ask Mary to do for you what she did at Cana and obtain for you a fresh outpouring of the Holy Spirit? Why can you count on Mary to hear you?

2. How often do you intercede for others? Ask Mary to teach you how to intercede.

3. The Holy Spirit is always given in superabundance, just as Jesus provided messianic abundance in the new wine. Bring to the Lord a bigger glass and ask him to fill it with his Spirit. Pray that he will increase your capacity to be filled with his Spirit. Then ask him how he wants you to serve others with the abundance you have received.

Chapter 14

More Children

Children are not supposed to die before their parents, but it happens all the time. As a priest I have prayed at the side of many a mother and father who have had their son or daughter snatched from their arms in untimely death. Sometimes the mother weeps silently; I have seen that often. At other times and in more expressive cultures, she screams. At a mortuary I stood beside the body of a thirty-year-old man who had just taken his life. When his mother arrived, she became hysterical, shook his body, and screamed, "Arnold, wake up, wake up!" Seeking to calm her, I placed my hand on her shoulder. All I could think to say was: "Emily, he will wake up, at the resurrection." (I have changed the names to protect the privacy of the mother and son.)

Filmmakers have portrayed Mary at Calvary in various ways, mostly in silent tears of grief. But in Zeffirelli's *Jesus of Nazareth,* when Jesus is taken from the cross and laid in her arms, she wails as she cradles him back and forth.

John tells us nothing of Mary's emotional state. It isn't necessary. As a consummate artist, he leaves it to the reader's imagination. As she stands by the cross, she is simply identified as "his mother." Enough said. It is Mary's ultimate act of letting go.

Had I been there, would my words, "He will wake up at the resurrection," have been any comfort to her? She already believed this, but what she doesn't know is that it will happen not at the end of time but three days later. For the time being, she is in the darkest sorrow. She is thirty years older now, maybe more, than when she made the trip to Ein Karem. That was not as long a journey—and certainly not as painful—as her climb to Calvary. Sister Isabel Bettwy, who has led many pilgrimages to Medjugorje, told me that on one of them, she was very concerned about an elderly lady in frail health. Knowing that one of the events of the pilgrimage—making the stations going up Cross Mountain—was quite strenuous, Sister Isabel told the woman that she could remain at the foot of the mountain and pray until the others returned. The woman replied, "Well, let me try." She made it to the fourth station, after which Sister intervened. "It gets very tough from here on. Wouldn't you rather wait here for us?" The lady thought for a moment, then smiled and said, "Well, Mary made it all the way." And so did Mary's frail daughter.

When Jesus' mother climbed that hill, she had no idea that it would inspire and give strength to generations to come. Though sorrow weighed upon every step, echoing the cross-laden steps of her son, the Holy Spirit empowered her. Her *fiat* at the annunciation brought the Holy Spirit to her heart and to her womb. Now the Holy Spirit whispers *fiat* in her heart and moves her steps to the summit.

Did Jesus' strength inspire hers, or did hers inspire his? There is a couple in our parish, Mary and Joe (their real names!), who give every moment they can spare to the church. Once a year, they prepare a Seder meal for the entire parish, which means a long day of labor before the meal, including being up most of the night cooking the lamb to its most tender state. At the meal,

I asked Mary if she was tired. "Well, yes," she said, "but when I get exhausted, I look into Mary's eyes, take a deep breath, and move on, just as Jesus did every time he fell."

What stunned me about her comment was that she said Jesus found strength in Mary's eyes. I would have thought it the other way around. Certainly Jesus was strong, physically and spiritually. He had learned how to be a man at the side of Joseph, the first one he called "Abba." Psychologists tell us that for healthy development, a boy must eventually detach himself from his natural dependence on his mother and identify with his father. Jesus certainly did that, and he said as much, as we saw in the previous chapter: "'Who is my mother and who are my brothers?' And pointing to his disciples, he said, 'Here are my mother and my brothers'" (Matthew 12:48-49). But Mary had become Jesus' mother already in that new sense, as disciple-companion of his mission, and if she understood the necessity of his going to the cross, her eyes would have said, "I have not taken back my *fiat,* just as you have not taken back yours in the garden." And in that resolve, Jesus would have found strength. Betrayed by one disciple, denied by another, abandoned by all, Jesus found strength is his mother's eyes. Knights used to fight battles for their ladies; Jesus fought to the end for Mary. He was paying the price for her immaculate conception, the first of the redeemed, and after her, the rest of us.

Mother to a Multitude

At the cross Jesus tells her that his Beloved Disciple is now her son and she, his mother. Now a whole new vista has opened, a whole new revelation, as Mary now accepts the disciple and his community as her children. What an exchange! A normal human mother would probably have rebelled at the replacement. But Mary has the Holy Spirit, and the Holy Spirit has a role in this birthing, just as he did in the birthing of Jesus. When Jesus breathes his last, John says, "He handed over the spirit" (John 19:30, NAB). A double meaning: It is his last human breath, but with it comes the Holy Spirit, for he is the breath of God. The Spirit, who came upon Mary at the angel's word to enflesh the Son of God, now comes upon her to effect the word of her firstborn: She is now mother of a "multitude of brothers" (Romans 8:29).

It is often said that Mary at the cross is an image of the Church as mother. That she is, for sure. But at the annunciation, she *was* the Church, the first and only believer. And at Cana, she believed before the disciples came to faith in Jesus. At the cross, is she not more than an image of mother Church? I think so. In this scene in which Jesus proclaims the Church as his family—the effect of his saving death—he addresses Mary first, then points to the disciple as her son. The relation Jesus creates is not just words, nor is Mary simply a cipher for the Church. Endowed with the Holy Spirit, when Jesus speaks, he creates what he says. When he tells the lame to walk, they walk; the blind to see, they see; the dead to rise, they rise. When he tells Mary that the disciple is her son, he *is* her son.

Such a transformation was already foretold at Cana when Jesus addressed his mother as "woman." She is the New Eve of Genesis and the new Mother Jerusalem birthing the new children of God. All that Cana promised is now fulfilled. We don't know if Jesus partook of the wine at Cana, but he did taste the cheap, sour wine on the cross, the wine of the poor and of soldiers. As he would replace the water of the Samaritan well with the living water of the Spirit, he would replace the sour wine of the cross with the new wine of the Holy Spirit.

But it is not only in his final breath that the Spirit is symbolized. The soldier's lance that pierces Jesus' side breaks a dam of blood and water. This double flow, dramatically pictured today in the Divine Mercy painting, is full of symbolism. The blood symbolizes the Eucharist. And the water? If Jesus' blood signifies one sacrament, then it is natural to think of the water as symbolizing another, baptism. But the water even more credibly symbolizes the Holy Spirit. For Jesus had cried out at the Feast of Tabernacles: "'If anyone thirsts, let him come to me and drink. The one who believes in me, as the Scripture says, from within him will flow rivers of living water.' He said this of the Spirit whom those who believed in him would receive" (John 7:37-39). From Jesus' body on the cross, those rivers of living water flowed.

This is John's painting of the mystery that Luke depicts at Pentecost. John ties the gift of the Spirit to Passover, indeed to the eve of Passover, when the Passover lambs were slain. As Mary will be with the disciples in the upper room when the Spirit comes, so is she with the handful of faithful disciples at the foot of the cross when Jesus gives them the Holy Spirit. Do these two portraits of the coming of the Spirit contradict one another? On the surface, it would seem so. But we must remember that in Jewish thought, Passover lasted fifty days, climaxing with Pentecost. John portrays the gift at the beginning of the season, Luke at the end. In both cases Jesus is the giver of the Holy Spirit, whether as the Passover Lamb or as the glorified and ascended Christ.

One Hour of Glory

The cross, then, is never separated from the mystery of the resurrection. That is why in John, Jesus breathes on his disciples both huddled at the cross and on Easter Sunday evening: "He breathed on them and said, 'Receive the Holy Spirit. Whose sins you forgive they are forgiven them; whose sins you retain, they are retained'" (John 20:22-23). Does John mean to say that there are two sendings of the Holy Spirit, one from the cross and one from the risen Jesus? No. Throughout his gospel Jesus refers to both the cross and the resurrection as one hour of glory for Jesus. The two scenes simply portray the two aspects of the gift of the Spirit: Both flow from the death and resurrection of Christ.

But John wants to show that the same Spirit has different effects, which he portrays in these two givings of the Spirit. At the cross Jesus formally establishes his new family, portraying Mary as its mother and sending the Holy Spirit to effect what he has just proclaimed. The emphasis is upon the new family that the risen Jesus will call his brothers and sisters (John 20:17). In the Easter evening scene, the Holy Spirit provides the newborn Church with authority, specifically the authority to forgive—or retain—sins. It is not too much to say that there is a beautiful complementarity in the double effect of the Spirit's gift: The Church is a family of brothers and sisters, but it also has an authority structure, as will become even clearer further on in the gospel, when Jesus commissions Peter to feed his sheep (John 21:15-17). The Church will have its authorized shepherds, and however imperfect, they will exercise their authority in the name of Jesus, but only to assure the unity and growth of the Church as family, gathered around its Mother. It is family that is primary, just as it is love that reigns over authority.

The Church ritualizes the relationship of authority to love in a simple, largely unrecognized liturgical way. In presiding at the Eucharist, the priest wears a stole and chasuble. In Roman times the stole stood for authority. The priest is to wear this symbol of his authority but only under the chasuble, which represents love, as St. Paul describes: "Over all these clothes put on love, which is the bond of perfection" (Colossians 3:14). Authority is subject to love. It is not the enemy of love but its guardian. That is why Mary and Peter stand as mainstays of the Church: Mary to show that we are family, Peter to assure its integrity.

....

Lord Jesus, how deep is the mystery of your love! With your mother and your Beloved Disciple, I stand at the foot of the cross, where I hear your voice proclaiming Mary as my mother too. And as the Holy Spirit made your words real, made them create the reality they signified, I ask that you breathe that same Holy Spirit upon me and flood me with the river of life-giving water that flows from your side. May I, too, experience Mary as my mother, letting her faith and love transform me, and may I see and love your Church as her family, yours, and mine. Amen.

FOR REFLECTION

1. In prayer put yourself at the foot of the cross as the Beloved Disciple, and relive the scene of John 19:25-37. What are your thoughts and feelings?

2. Why is it essential that the Church be both family and have an authority structure?

3. When you get tired, how can you find strength by looking into the eyes of Mary?

Chapter 15

Outpouring

We switch our lens back to St. Luke as we open his second book, the Acts of the Apostles. After Jesus' ascension, the apostles gather in the upper room. "All these devoted themselves with one accord to prayer, together with some women, and Mary the mother of Jesus, and his brothers" (Acts 1:14, NAB). The mention of Mary invites a flashback to the infancy stories in which Mary played a major role. Her role here in Acts is much more discrete, as this is the only mention of her in the whole book. But having first shown us a domestic Pentecost, Luke now shows us the universal gift of the Spirit.

Each word of Acts 1:14 tells us something. Who are "all these"? They are the eleven apostles (Matthias, the replacement for Judas, will be added shortly). Luke has just listed them in the preceding verse. The Church is going to be built on these foundation stones, as the Apocalypse will note: "The wall of the city [the heavenly Jerusalem] had twelve courses of stones as its foundation, on which were inscribed the twelve names of the twelve apostles of the Lamb" (Revelation 21:14, NAB). Luke will make it abundantly clear that while the Holy Spirit is leading the community, it is under the earthly authority of the apostles.

This community is first of all a community of prayer. The phrase "All these devoted themselves" tells us that they did more than say a few occasional prayers; they dropped everything and gave themselves to prayer with intensity and perseverance. We can imagine that many fasted, and it is likely that prayer continued through the night watches, with people taking shifts to pray while others broke to eat or sleep. And they did this "with one accord," all united, the apostles and Mary, in this urgent preparation for the gift of the Holy Spirit. Having experienced her Pentecost at the annunciation, Mary was doubtless the one who inspired this first intercessory prayer of the gathered Church. Paul would later say that the Holy Spirit intercedes within the Christian "with inexpressible groanings" (Romans 8:26). Inasmuch as the rest of the community had not yet received this outpouring of the Spirit, they must have looked to Mary to show them how to pray in the Spirit in this way. The gift of the Holy Spirit would be new for the disciples. For Mary it would bring a deeper union with her Spouse, a new departure, a new expansion of love.

These days of preparation for Pentecost contain an important lesson. Our ability to receive the Holy Spirit is in proportion to our intense desire and preparation for him. How big a container will we bring to this "Niagara Falls"? A thimble or a barrel? He will always overflow whatever container we bring, because the gift goes beyond the measure of preparation. But we choose the size of the container.

And so it happened. A powerful wind shook the house, and fire like that consuming the sacrifice of Elijah descended upon the hundred and twenty: "tongues as of fire, which parted and came to rest on each one of them" (Acts 2:3, NAB). "Parted" indicates that the fire appeared as a single column of flame that then divided and dispersed to each. One wonders if the column did not descend first on Mary and then disperse to the rest. "All were filled with the holy Spirit and began to speak in different tongues" (2:4). That would have included Mary. Not even her Magnificat could adequately express what was happening. Like the rest, she burst into syllables she had never used before, not understanding what she was saying but knowing that she was caught up in an embrace that transcended words. This must have gone on long enough for a crowd of pilgrims from different countries to gather outside and listen. And suddenly each listener heard a message meant for him and his people—a forecast of the Church's world mission! Most listeners were astounded, but some said the noise sounded like the bar songs of drunks. "They have had too much new wine" (2:13, NAB). Indeed, it was the new wine that old wine skins could not contain, the wine of the Holy Spirit.

Sober Intoxication

From his "sober intoxication," Peter recovers sufficiently to open the second-floor window and speak to the crowds. "We're not drunk, as some of you think. How could we be? It's only nine o'clock in the morning! There is a touch of humor here, because people usually "get drunk at night" (1 Thessalonians 5:7). But there is a deeper meaning here. Whether or not Peter recalled it, it was in the morning that the great theophany took place on Mount Sinai (Exodus 19:16) with fire and smoke. That heralded the gift of the law. The fire of Pentecost heralded the gift of the Spirit.

Mary remains in the background as the early Church develops under the leadership of the apostles. She is no doubt there when, after Peter and John were hauled before the Sanhedrin, the community went into prayer again and experienced a "second

Pentecost," emboldening the apostles to speak the word of God fearlessly (Acts 4:23-31). Prayer and intercession will be her role throughout the rapid-fire action of Acts. She is not involved in the decisions of the apostles. She leaves that to them and the Holy Spirit ("The Holy Spirit and we have decided," Acts 15:28), but she pleads incessantly for every new outpouring of the Spirit that is needed in the tumultuous development of the Church. It is, after all, her family, and what Christian mother does not pray for her children?

She was no doubt part of the Jewish church in Jerusalem for a time, but tradition has it that John took her to Ephesus, the disciple's base of operations. Today you can visit a "House of Mary" up in the hills above Ephesus commemorating her home there, presumably where the assumption occurred. But there is also a first-century tomb in the Kedron Valley in Jerusalem that some have claimed as the tomb of Mary.

In defining the doctrine of the assumption of Mary, Pope Pius XII did not specify whether Mary actually died or whether she was taken up into heavenly glory without dying. Theologically speaking, because she was free of original sin, the cause of death according to Genesis, she did not have to die. We don't know whether she experienced physical death or whether she was taken directly into heaven while still alive, as Paul says will happen to those living at the time of the Lord's return (1 Thessalonians 4:16-17; 1 Corinthians 15:51). But if her son had died, would she not have wanted to be one in his sacrifice by experiencing death? Even if she had not died, she would have been bodily transformed in a glory like that of her son. In heaven she takes on a new form of ministry, as we shall see in the next chapter.

....

Lord Jesus, give me the kind of hunger and thirst for your Holy Spirit that Mary and the early disciples had as they awaited the coming of the Holy Spirit. Expand my capacity to receive. May Mary, who grew each day in your love, show me how to grow in my own life. And may the Holy Spirit visit your Church today with a new Pentecost to draw all people into your kingdom. Amen.

FOR REFLECTION

1. Mary's role at Pentecost was a prayerful presence. When I am not chosen for a leadership position, am I willing to serve happily in a more hidden way?

2. Mary and the disciples prepared for Pentecost by intense prayer. Do I eagerly prepare for the great feasts of the liturgical year with prayer, novenas, fasting, or sacrifices so that my capacity can grow to receive the graces of those feasts?

3. In asking for a renewal of the Holy Spirit in my life, have I asked Mary to teach me how to prepare and how to receive?

Chapter 16

Glory

Even though led by the Holy Spirit, Mary during her earthly life lived by faith and not by sight (2 Corinthians 5:7). But once she is assumed into heavenly glory, she sees God face-to-face, and in him she sees all that God wants her to see, in its totality with perfect clarity. The Spirit's candlelight in her night walk of faith gives way to the light of day, and her intercession, likewise moved by the Holy Spirit, shares in the intercessory power of her glorified son.

When you are reading the Apocalypse and turn the page from chapter 11 to 12, you are suddenly confronted with a sign in the sky: "a woman clothed with the sun, with the moon under her feet and on her head a crown of twelve stars" (Revelation 12:1, NAB). Who is this woman? She is both the Church and Mary, like the overlay of two photographs or a movie that shows you two scenes, one superimposed over the other. On the one hand, the woman is glorious, vested with divine light; on the other, she is on earth, threatened in her pregnancy by the dragon, Satan. She brings forth a child who is then "caught up to God and his throne" (12:5, NAB). Her child here is doubtless Jesus, and his rapture refers to his ascension into heavenly glory. The woman is both glorious and suffering, both pursued and protected, and hence is an image of both the Church here on earth and the Church in heaven in glory.

Though the Church has not used this text to prove the assumption of Mary, she does use this scene in the liturgy of the feast. So we are invited to contemplate the role of Mary both in glory and somehow also at one with the Church struggling on earth, what we call the "Church Militant." She is the mother of the Messiah but also the mother of her other children (Revelation 12:17) who continue the struggle with Satan on earth.

This intimate union of the Church in glory with the Church on earth runs throughout the Apocalypse. The author shows us a split screen, the upper one portraying what is happening in heaven, the lower one portraying what is happening on earth, and these two are closely related. Now Mary in glory embodies the Church in glory but also the Church's concern for those still struggling with Satan on earth. That is why her role, like that of all the saints in glory, is prayerful intercession for her children still at war.

And this intercession is effective. The prayers of the saints go up like incense before God, and in response God intervenes on earth on behalf of his suffering people (Revelation 8:3-5). As Queen Mother now occupying a throne next to her son, she is, of all the saints, the primary intercessor, for that was the role of the Queen Mother in the Old Testament's portrayal of her. So it is with good reason that in prayer, after repeating to Mary the angel's words and those of Elizabeth blessing Mary, we say, "Holy Mary, Mother of God, pray for us sinners . . ."

Messenger and Evangelizer

But in God's scheme of things, Mary is more than an intercessor in heaven. She is a messenger on earth as well. Granted that all God wanted to say is contained in the Bible and in the revelation given to the apostles, yet the voice of prophecy continues in the Church, bringing the word of God to life with a here-and-now urgency—and Mary leads the charge. I refer to the apparitions in which Mary is the chosen spokesperson of the Holy Spirit. I mean, of course, those apparitions judged by the Church to be authentic, such as Lourdes and Fatima, and those elsewhere approved by the local bishops, such as Kibeho in Rwanda and Betania in Venezuela. In these apparitions the Virgin Mary is simply but powerfully proclaiming the gospel call to conversion, prayer, penance, and holiness. She continues to lead to Jesus.

But notice how she always appears as a woman of the ethnic stock of the people where the apparitions happen. At Lourdes she appeared as a beautiful French woman, in Kibeho as a Rwandan, in Mexico as a mestiza—the latter, perhaps, coming closest to how a young Galilean woman might have looked. Notice that the Guadalupe image portrays her as pregnant. Centuries earlier Mary was pregnant for nine months, but this could not have been her condition at the time of her apparition. All of this shows us that apparitions are artistic creations of the Holy Spirit mediating a presence of the Mother of God in a form that the local visionary and the people can instantly identify with. "Am I not your mother?" she said to Juan Diego, and she looked like kin.

The point of this is that the Holy Spirit, who continues the work of Jesus in the Church, uses Mary as the great evangelizer. It is not only her apparitions but her message that evangelizes. And that message is none other than Jesus' own gospel message, which begins with a call to repentance. Why does the Holy Spirit choose Mary rather than Jesus or some other form by which to communicate his message? Some apparitions, of course, have been of Jesus, as, for example, the Sacred Heart of Jesus to St. Margaret Mary Alacoque or Jesus the Divine Mercy to St. Faustina. But the majority of apparitions have been of Mary.

God is free, of course, to do as he pleases, but we are permitted to ask if there is some method to the madness of his love for us that prompts his continued interventions in time and space, and to intervene mostly through Mary. Is it that our human hearts more easily identify with Mary, a pure creature who is not God and is at the same time mother, the closest of all human relationships? Before World War I, my Uncle Laurie had been working in Mexico, far from his home in Texas. One night at supper in a cantina, he heard the mariachis play "La Golondrina," the song of a homesick man who sees a swallow flying to his homeland where he can't go. The image of his mother flashed before Laurie's mind. His own pent-up homesickness welled up in tears, and he got up and started home to see his mother. Such is the appeal of a mother to human heartstrings. Such is the appeal of our mother Mary too. She is also closest to us because she walks by faith and not by sight, as do the rest of us. She has struggled in the darkness of unknowing, as do we. She models receptivity to the mysterious actions of God in our lives, some of which involve suffering.

Spiritual Companion

There is yet another way the Holy Spirit brings Mary into our lives, and that is as spiritual companion. The Holy Spirit dwells in us, not merely in a static way, as the image of a spiritual temple might suggest (1 Corinthians 3:17), but in a dynamic way, as other images suggest: breath, wind, fire, living water. He fosters continual growth until we attain to full maturity in Christ (Ephesians 4:7-16). We also know that great saints have practiced a kind of spiritual union with Mary and have promoted it among the faithful. St. Louis-Marie Grignion de Montfort's *True Devotion to the Blessed Virgin* continues to have a profound influence on the faithful. It was Pope John Paul II's favorite book for spiritual reading. As he stepped out on the balustrade after his election as pope, he shouted out *"Totus Tuus"* ("I am all yours") as a rallying battle cry for the future of the Church. A laywoman friend of mine has had a close sense of the presence of Mary for many years, at times sensing a directive word from her.

These people are but three shamrock leaves in a field of millions who have had spiritual experiences of Mary. How do you explain the fact that Mary, the simple little maiden of Nazareth, could have such a vast, almost universal influence? She is, after all, a limited human being. We can understand how Jesus, being God, could choose to grant a spiritual experience of himself at any time or place, and even in multiple places at the same time. But Mary? The only explanation that makes sense is that the indwelling Holy Spirit, who has no face of his own, brings Mary to the consciousness of the Christian, enabling in many cases a real dialogue between the Mother of God and the human person. The union of Mary and the Holy Spirit, begun at the annunciation, continues now with Mary in glory—and in the heart where the Holy Spirit dwells. And now, as then, Mary and the Holy Spirit form Jesus in us.

Unifier

Finally, Mary is an instrument of the Holy Spirit in fostering the unity of the Church. Paul speaks of "the unity of the Spirit in the bond of peace—one body and one Spirit" (Ephesians 4:3-4), and he prays that the fellowship, the union, created by the Holy Spirit will bless his readers (2 Corinthians 13:13). As mother, Mary wants to make the Church family. Many people think of the Church as a mere institution with authority and rules. No, the Church is a family, a family that has a mother. And in it we all are equally brothers and sisters. The old divisions have been abolished (Galatians 3:28; Ephesians 2:14). We have God as our father and Mary as our mother and a multitude as brothers and sisters (Romans 8:29).

What are the consequences of this? In a small prayer group in Kathmandu, Nepal, we decided to share what each one of us considered the heaviest cross in our life. A mother said she suffered most when her children were not at peace with one another. If you are at odds with any of your brothers or sisters (and here I mean not only blood siblings but your siblings in Christ), then look what it is doing to your mother. Is it any wonder that in many of her apparitions, Mary is shedding tears?

Mary in glory, Mary in tears. The Church in glory, the Church in tears. The good news is that one phase is temporary, the other eternal. While we struggle, the Holy Spirit through Mary empowers us to walk as she did, through the night of faith into the day of everlasting glory.

....

Mary, I turn to you, my mother wrapped in the sun of glory, and beg your intercession for my needs and the needs of your struggling children on earth. Though you are in heaven, walk with us on earth through the indwelling Holy Spirit to light our path and bring us safely home. Amen.

FOR REFLECTION

1. Reflect on what it means that Mary always appears as a woman of the local people. What does this say about the Holy Spirit's use of her for evangelization?

2. We are engaged in spiritual warfare because we are the "rest of her children" against whom the dragon wages war (Revelation 12:17). What are our weapons? What were Mary's?

3. How familiar are you with the messages that Mary delivered in the apparitions approved by the Church, such as Lourdes, Fatima, and La Salette? How can meditating on those messages help you grow in your faith?

Chapter 17

The Spirit
and the Bride

The Spirit and the bride say, 'Come!'" (Revelation 22:17, NAB). This signature to the Book of Revelation shows the Spirit and the bride calling in one harmonizing song of divine beauty. We close this book, then, listening to the duet that closes the Bible itself.

The Spirit is the Holy Spirit. But who is the bride? She is the Church, as we learn when the angel tells John, "Come here. I will show you the bride, the wife of the Lamb" (Revelation 21:9-10, NAB). We expect to see a beautiful woman, perhaps the woman of chapter 12 robed with the sun, crowned with stars, with the moon under her feet. But surprise! We see instead the holy city, the New Jerusalem, coming down out of heaven from God. This is the Church in splendor gradually coming to realization on earth. The Church is the bride, the wife of the Lamb. The collectivity is imaged as a woman.

Are the Spirit and the bride in heaven or on earth? The meaning that immediately comes to mind in the cry "Come!" is the Church Militant here on earth, inspired by the Holy Spirit to ask the Lord to come and come quickly—*Maranatha!* For the Lord has just said twice that he is coming soon (22:7, 12). But the bride in chapter 22 is the heavenly Church, the Church in glory. So it is equally possible that the Holy Spirit and the bride in glory are inviting the faithful to "Come!" And the sequence suggests what they are to come for: "the gift of life-giving water" (22:17, NAB). It doesn't take a great deal of imagination to think that the heavenly Church's "Come" is her response to the earthly Church's "Come." It's as if the heavenly Church is saying that the way for you to experience the coming of the Lord right now is to come forward yourself and receive the Holy Spirit, gift of life-giving water and earthly foretaste of the glory to come.

If it is the Church in glory who says to us, "Come," then we know that the woman who has already, body and soul, become the paradigm of the Church in glory, Mary, is the leading voice in this invitation. The Second Vatican Council says as much: "In the most holy virgin the Church has already reached that perfection whereby she exists 'without spot or wrinkle' (cf. Ephesians 5:27)" (*Lumen Gentium*, 65). Thus, with the Holy Spirit, she sings to us the duet, "Come!"

Such is the fitting climax of what we have contemplated all along. Mary, on earth singing with the Holy Spirit the duet of invitation and response, now in glory joins the Holy Spirit in inviting the earthly Church to respond as she did during her night of faith. Short of the vision of glory, the Church now drinks of the life-giving water of the Spirit, who offers provisional relief to her thirst for the kingdom.

....

Holy Spirit, you are the love song of love songs. Awaken in me the total loving response you awakened in Mary. Mary, teach me the part you sing in this love song. I know that my voice is not as pure as yours. But I also know that the Holy Spirit came to you, not just for you, but for me and the rest of us, so that you might teach us how to harmonize our hearts and our lives with the Holy Spirit. And may we who struggle to sing against the competing noises of this world one day join you and the choir of all the blessed in that perfect concert begun long ago in your heart here on earth. Amen.

For Reflection

1. As you finish this book, what are some of the major insights that remain with you?

About the Author

 Fr. George Montague, SM, a Marianist priest, was born and grew up on a Texas ranch, from which he often makes parables of his experiences. Ordained a priest in 1958, he received his doctorate in biblical studies from the University of Fribourg in Switzerland in 1960. He has served his community in various ministries: as professor of Scripture at St. Mary's University for thirty-one years, as seminary rector in St. Louis and Toronto, and as director of Indian Marianist novices in Kathmandu, Nepal. Former president of the Catholic Biblical Association of America and editor of the *Catholic Biblical Quarterly*, he is the author of two dozen books on Scripture and spirituality. He is also cofounder of a new religious community of priests and brothers, the Brothers of the Beloved Disciple.

the **WORD**
among us ®
The *Spirit* of Catholic Living

This book was published by The Word Among Us. For nearly thirty years, The Word Among Us has been answering the call of the Second Vatican Council to help Catholic laypeople encounter Christ in the Scriptures—a call reiterated recently by Pope Benedict XVI and a Synod of Bishops.

The name of our company comes from the prologue to the Gospel of John and reflects the vision and purpose of all of our publications: to be an instrument of the Spirit, whose desire it is to manifest Jesus' presence in and to the children of God. In this way, we hope to contribute to the Church's ongoing mission of proclaiming the gospel to the world and growing ever more deeply in our love for the Lord.

Our monthly devotional magazine, *The Word Among Us*, features meditations on the daily and Sunday Mass readings, and currently reaches more than one million Catholics in North America each year and another 500,000 Catholics in 100 countries. Our press division has published nearly 200 books and Bible studies over the past 12 years.

To learn more about who we are and what we publish, log on to our Web site at **www.wau.org**. There you will find a variety of Catholic resources that will help you grow in your faith.

Embrace His Word, Listen to God . . .

www.wau.org